✓ B + J
3/8/85
23.95

RETHINKING COGNITIVE THEORY

This book is a sequel to Jeff Coulter's *The Social Construction of Mind* and is an attack on dominant trends in cognitive science and the philosophy of psychology from an ethnomethodological/ Wittgensteinian standpoint. Coulter argues the case for a sociological or social constructionist approach to mind and therefore undermines recent attempts to reduce the philosophy of mind to the study of states of the brain or central nervous system, the "neuroscientific" view of how people think.

Contemporary approaches to human cognition are usually formulated in terms of a computational model. This book examines a range of assumptions and theses characteristic of this way of thinking about the human mind. Among the topics discussed are: the doctrine of psychophysiological determinism; cognitive "information-processing" theory; anomalous monism; storage models of memory; "rule-governed" conduct; the relationship of language to experience; the prospects for a social-constructionist framework for cognitive analysis, and the general problem of "natural kinds" in the study of the mental and experiential life.

This is a fully professional, useful, clearly written and competent book. The treatment is scholarly and well-referenced.

Jeff Coulter is Associate Professor of Sociology and faculty member of the Division of Linguistic Behavior of the Graduate School of Arts and Sciences, Boston University. He is the author of *Approaches to Insanity* (1974) and *The Social Construction of Mind* (1979) in addition to numerous papers dealing with issues in the philosophy of the behavioral sciences.

RETHINKING COGNITIVE THEORY

Jeff Coulter

St. Martin's Press   New York

All rights reserved. For information, write:
St. Martin's Press, Inc., 175 Fifth Avenue, New York, NY 10010
Printed in Hong Kong
Published in the United Kingdom by The Macmillan Press Ltd.
First published in the United States of America in 1983

ISBN 0-312-67800-2

Library of Congress Cataloging in Publication Data

Coulter, Jeff.
  Rethinking cognitive theory.

  Sequel to: The social construction of mind. 1979.
  Bibliography: p.
  Includes index.
  1. Cognition — Philosophy.   2. Psychology — Philosophy.
3. Wittgenstein, Ludwig, 1889-1951.   I. Title.
BF311.C7   1983   153.4   83-9639
ISBN 0-312-67800-2

For My Daughter
JINAN

'. . . there is no reason (for sociologists) to look under the skull since nothing of interest is to be found there but brains.'

Harold Garfinkel, 'A Conception of, and Experiments with, "Trust" as a Condition of Stable Concerted Actions', in O.J. Harvey (ed.), *Motivation and Social Interaction* (N.Y.: Ronald Press, 1963) p. 190.

'. . . it is unlikely that the brain is organized into systems that fit our labels.'

Elliot S. Valenstein, *Brain Control: A Critical Examination of Brain Stimulation and Psychosurgery* (N.Y.: John Wiley, 1973) p. 131.

Contents

Preface

In this work, I attempt to deepen and broaden the philosophical approach to the study of cognition outlined and defended in my book, *The Social Construction of Mind* (Macmillan: London, 1979; New Jersey: Rowman & Littlefield, 1979). In some respects, then, this may be treated as a kind of sequel to that work. My general purpose here is to subject an array of theoretical positions in cognitive studies to logical analysis with the objective of establishing the relevance of a synthesis of Wittgensteinian and ethnomethodological analysis, here referred to as 'conceptual phenomenology'.

The professional reader will discern at once that, whilst I am entirely sympathetic to the transcendence of narrowly behaviouristic approaches to human conduct and reasoning, I am out of sympathy with many of the positions which have been advanced to replace the old paradigms of analysis. The student who picks up this book will find ideas and arguments here not usually encountered in his cognitive and social psychology readings; if he is a student of philosophy (especially of the philosophy of mind and action), he will find various themes taken from the analytic tradition and put to work on theoretical schemes available in the contemporary behavioural sciences with which he may not be familiar. This is, then, a critical and integrative series of studies in so far as it brings into relation arguments from very diverse sources. The significance of trying to do this in the service of reconstructing the epistemological bases of cognitive analysis is, I hope, worth the effort. There are, of course, many topics not treated here, or not treated in an exhaustive way. Nonetheless, I have tried to tackle a variety of issues which are, I believe, fundamental to the field. These include: the computational theory of conduct; psychophysiological determinism; 'cognitive' information-processing theory; token physicalism and anomalous monism as they relate to neuro-psychology; the relationship of 'rules' to human conduct; theoretical models of human memory; sentient automata theory as a general metaphysics of modern cognitive studies; the problem of analysing the experiences of non-linguistic and pre-linguistic organisms; the relationship of language to experience; the prospects for a social-interactional view of topics in cognitive science, and the limits of operationalism and hypostatisation in studies of schizophrenia and intelligence (two polar concepts in our 'mental' vocabulary).

This book, then, is an exercise in the philosophy of the behavioural sciences. It is written in large measure to satisfy many colleagues and students familiar with my general views who have urged me to set them out in a more systematic fashion than is permitted during the course of lectures and seminars. As in my previous book on mind, I sketch here some research-guiding arguments and attempt to illustrate their cogency with worked examples. A critic of a (currently) dominant mode of thought had better be prepared to practise what he preaches, even if he cannot do the whole job alone.

I have presented arguments in public forums and colloquia on some of these issues since the *Mind* study. A preliminary assessment of the mind/brain identity thesis and corollary versions of 'thinking', 'thought' and 'recognition' was published under the title: 'The Brain as Agent' in *Human Studies* , vol. 2, no. 4, 1979. In that discussion, I confined myself to *type* physicalist versions of the relationship of mind to brain; in these essays, it is *token* physicalism with which I am more concerned. A first attempt to trace some of the implications of the Wittgensteinian conception of the mental for developments in Turing-machine functionalist psychology was presented on 27 January 1981 to the Boston Colloquium for the Philosophy of Science at Boston University, where Professor Daniel Dennett kindly agreed to argue with me about some of the theses advanced in his book, *Brainstorms*. My preoccupation with several of the arguments in that stimulating work is evident again in the first chapter of this book. My paper delivered at the Colloquium is available in the journal *Inquiry*, vol. 25, no. 1, 1982 under the title: 'Theoretical Problems of Cognitive Science'.

Although I have sought to document fully my indebtedness to those philosophers whose writings continue to inspire me in this effort – in particular, Norman Malcolm, John F.M. Hunter, David E. Cooper and P.M.S. Hacker – there are other debts which resist detailed attribution. In particular, I would like to thank my mentor for so many years, Wes Sharrock, for having introduced me to the importance of Wittgenstein for conceptual clarification in the behavioural sciences, and for having kept up a lively correspondence with me on these issues in the midst of many other demands upon his time. Whilst there may well be much in what follows with which none of these thinkers could agree, I hope that what I have learned from them all shows through these pages.

I have also greatly benefited from the intellectual community of members of the Boston University Interaction Research Group who have tolerated my abstract preoccupations, and who have shown in their own work the vitality of the ethnomethodological paradigm. To George Psathas, Rich Frankel, Tim Anderson, David Holm, Jay Meehan, Paul Jalbert, Marty Sawzin, Anne Rawls, Cliff Michel, Rolf Diamon, Paula Swilling, Joel Kallich, Amy Neustein: thank you all. Thanks are due to Kathy Blackwell for the preparation of this book for publication. I should also like to thank my remarkable mother-in-law, Professor Salma K. Jayyusi, who, although eminent in a very different field, inspired me in difficult times with her enthusiasm and zest for work, and my wife, Lena Jayyusi, whose love and intellectual partnership I value deeply.

JEFF COULTER
Boston University, 1982

Introduction

A variety of interrelated theoretical problems arising out of the study of cognition are examined in this book. At the heart of many of these problems are recurrent programmatic claims about the appropriateness of conceiving of human 'cognitive conduct' in terms of conceptual schemes borrowed from computer science. The 'computational' theory of mind and behaviour, and the related notions of persons as 'information-processing systems' and 'sentient automata', informs a great deal of contemporary research and theory construction in the field. As many commentators have noted,[1] the leading alternative to behaviouristic strategies of description and explanation these days is some form of 'cognitive' model of conduct, and this is increasingly the case not only within human psychology, but within theoretical linguistics, philosophy of mind and action, microsociology and anthropology. Indeed, since the celebrated Chomsky–Skinner debate of the late nineteen fifties, one can trace a polarisation among theoreticians in the human sciences, if not a full-blown case of a 'paradigm-shift'.

These intellectual developments have not been without their detractors. Early shots were fired from such diverse quarters as phenomenological philosophy, with Dreyfus's controversial critiques of work in the field of 'artificial intelligence',[2] Black's and Quine's attempts to rebut Chomskian cognitivism in linguistic theory,[3] and Weizenbaum's discussion of the limits of relevance of artificial-intelligence research to human problems,[4] a critique emanating from a distinguished practitioner of such research. In recent years, many ordinary-language philosophers have sought to specify the precise nature of the inferences which may be drawn from work in the fields of 'cognitive psychology'

1

and 'psycholinguistics' along computational lines in terms of its relevance to the illumination of human conduct. Here, the writings of Malcolm,[5] Hunter[6] and Cooper[7] have been among the most significant. However, there is little doubt that those working in the newly established tradition of 'cognitive' studies have dismissed such detractors as either 'neo-behaviourists'[8] or as simply engaged in a passé form of 'linguistic analysis' which may safely be ignored by hard-nosed researchers.

I have argued elsewhere against the view that a critical analysis of cognitive theorising commits one to *any* form of behaviouristic alternative as that label is normally used in psychology. Indeed, the present theoretical obstacles confronting developments in the study of cognition can only be surmounted if, once and for all, the contributions of the Wittgensteinian tradition in the philosophy of mind are adequately appreciated and no longer misassimilated to behaviourism of any kind. For behaviourism resolutely refused to recognise the constitutive nature of language and culture for the very availability of 'what a person is doing', and its reductionist biases toward treating actions and motoric events as identical *explananda* prevented it from appreciating the richness of our everyday, pre-theoretical ways of describing human doings. On the other hand, the present exaggerated emphases on the 'unconscious', the 'inner workings' of a 'mind', stand in dire need of correction from an intellectual tradition in which the logic of 'mental' concepts and predicates in a public language was being worked out. These are themes which I shall take up in connection with various topics in the following pages.

The basic position of this book may be stated in four propositions. Firstly, that whatever pass for 'cognitive' phenomena have integral relationships, logically, to features of the publicly available life-world. Secondly, that most of the present difficulties facing cognitive theory can at least be illuminated by a closer inspection and critique of its conceptual assumptions. Thirdly, that such a critique furnishes a basis for a fuller understanding of the socio-cultural properties of 'the mental' and contributes to a necessary process of theoretical dereification. And fourthly, that a viable 'praxiological' foundation for studies of cognition in everyday life-worlds is possible. In developing these arguments, I have also sought to specify, where relevant, the relationship between my own social-constructionist orientation to cognitive analysis and the domain of the (neuro-) physiological.

If the many arguments presented here can stimulate further discussion, the effort will have been worthwhile, for I do not claim to have done more in these pages than to have set out my own reasons for dissatisfaction with prevailing orthodoxies, along with some attempt at reformulating recalcitrant problems. Nonetheless, I think that the *kind* of arguments advanced, and the traditions from which they emerge, preserve intact the goal of all students of cognition: the possibility of a scientific approach to the study of the properties of 'mind'. The differences lie in how we conceive of that project.

NOTES

1. An early but useful discussion is to be found in D. S. Palermo, 'Is A Scientific Revolution Taking Place in Psychology?' *Science Studies*, vol. 1, no. 1, pp. 135–55.
2. H. L. Dreyfus, *Alchemy and Artificial Intelligence* (Santa Monica, Ca: Rand Corporation, 1965) and *What Computers Can't Do: A Critique of Artificial Reason* (New York: Harper & Row, 1972). Seymour Papert's somewhat frenzied response to Dreyfus's first book, *The Artificial Intelligence of Hubert L. Dreyfus* (Cambridge, Mass.: M.I.T. AI Lab., 1968), whilst making some reasonable points (and some unreasonable ones as well) loses itself in its propensity for diatribe. That such polemics are still forthcoming from cognitive scientists confronted with reasoned arguments (which may, of course, turn out to be wrong) is a sad fact about some of the interchanges which have taken place over the years. Chomsky's replies to some of his critics in *Behavioral and Brain Sciences*, vol. 3, no. 1 (March 1980) struck me as unnecessarily harsh in tone, as did the Lachmans' review of my own earlier work in *Contemporary Psychology* (June 1981) in which I was accused of relying upon Wittgenstein's works as a Rosetta stone for unlocking every problem in psychology. It did not strike the Lachmans as even a remote possibility that what Wittgenstein had to say about various topics I dealt with might merit some careful attention. Sometimes, it seems as though an argument is only an argument when it is advanced by a cognitivist; when advanced by a critic, it becomes merely a 'polemic'. Perhaps some of us critics have been guilty of all this as well, however, on occasion. Cognitive studies are nothing if not committed, it appears.
3. Max Black, 'Comment on Chomsky's "Explanation in Linguistic Theory" '

in R. Borger and F. Cioffi (eds), *Explanation in the Behavioural Sciences* (Cambridge: Cambridge University Press, 1970). W. V. Quine, 'Methodological Reflections on Linguistic Theory' in D. Davidson and G. Harman (eds), *Semantics of Natural Language* (Boston: D. Riedel, Humanities Press, 1972).

4. Joseph Weizenbaum, *Computer Power and Human Reason: From Judgment to Calculation* (San Francisco: Freeman, 1976).

5. Norman Malcolm, 'The Myth of Cognitive Processes and Structures' in T. Mischel (ed.), *Cognitive Development and Epistemology* (New York: Academic Press, 1971).

6. J. F. M. Hunter, 'On How We Talk' in his *Essays After Wittgenstein* (Toronto: University of Toronto Press, 1973).

7. David E. Cooper, *Knowledge of Language* (New York: Humanities Press, 1975).

8. W. F. Brewer, in his paper, 'The Problem of Meaning and the Interrelations of the Higher Mental Processes', in Walter B. Weimer and David S. Palermo (eds), *Cognition and the Symbolic Processes* (New York: Erlbaum/Halsted/John Wiley, 1974) remarks on what he terms 'the philosophy of language' (although from his references to Malcolm's work it is clear he means 'ordinary-language philosophy' as a whole) and comments that it 'still appears to be wandering around in the wastelands of Behaviorism'. (pp. 289–90). He quotes Malcolm (see my ref. 5 above) as saying: 'Thus, it is the facts, the circumstances surrounding that behavior, that give it the property of expressing recognition (– not an act or process, over and above, or behind, the expression of recognition)' and construes this as a behaviouristic claim. It seems to me that it is nothing of the sort. Although it denies a constitutive role for 'mental' or 'cognitive' acts or processes in relation to what 'recognition' actually amounts to, it does not reduce recognition to a set of 'responses' or mere behavioural events of an organism. Malcolm is saying that contextual particulars constitute behaviours *as* instances of, *inter alia*, recognising someone.

1 On the epistemological foundations of cognitive science

For those who believe that the best work in artificial-intelligence research promises to deliver a coherent and decidable 'theory of mind', the following remarks from a prominent practitioner may have a salutary effect:

> [T]he problem is that a unique abstract characterization of man's cognitive functioning does not exist. . . . The fact that it is not possible to uniquely determine cognitive structures and processes poses a clear limitation on our ability to understand the nature of human intelligence. I once thought it could mean unique identification of the structures and processes underlying cognitive behavior. Since that is not possible, I propose that we take 'understanding the nature of human intelligence' to mean possession of a theory that will enable us to improve human intelligence.[1]

Although John Anderson's view may not (yet) embody a disciplinary consensus, it is instructive and refreshingly open about the field within which he works. Of course, this is far from claiming that artificial-intelligence research *as a whole* has been oriented toward a goal such as he describes. Indeed, there are many practitioners for whom theoretical questions about 'cognition' are less relevant, interesting or important than endogenous programming and hardware problems generated by attempts to construct simulations of complex tasks of whatever

5

kind. However, before we indulge in any general kind of scepticism about studies of cognition, it is worthwhile to reconsider the fundamental questions which motivated the field and to ask about them: were they well-formed research questions? is it essential for studies of cognition to postulate 'underlying' structures and processes (where 'underlying' means something like: realised in the brain or 'mind')? are such postulates even *in principle* coherent?

Jerry Fodor has sought to defend the metatheoretical position of 'computational' cognitivism, claiming that:

> it seems to be implicit in almost every kind of explanation that cognitive psychologists accept [that] behavior [is] the outcome of computation, and computation presupposes a medium in which to compute. But, on the other hand, the assumption of such a medium is relatively rarely made explicit.[2]

Since Fodor's is widely held to be the best elaborated philosophical defence of the computational approach to studies of cognition and conduct, it is worthy of detailed consideration. I want to argue that, if Fodor's defence (and elaboration) of a computational theory of conduct is untenable (which I believe to be the case), then, in the light of Anderson's view expressed above, we should perhaps locate some solid grounds for proposing alternative perspectives. In fact, I think that Anderson too hastily urges us to jettison a theoretical interest in cognition in favour of a practical, applied orientation to the topic. However, my own view of what is involved in developing a theoretical 'understanding of the nature of human intelligence' must be put aside for the moment until we have seen whether or not there are grounds for endorsing the sort of programme advanced by Fodor.

1 FODOR'S COMPUTATIONAL-REPRESENTATION THEORY OF 'COGNITIVE' CONDUCT

Fodor's is a rich and variegated treatment of the problems raised by the computational approach to human cognition, and a full appraisal of his many arguments would require a study almost as long as his original. What I propose to attempt here is a selective critique of his fundamental arguments, and a more or less 'shot-gun' approach to some secondary or derivative claims which are to varying degrees based upon those fundamental arguments. It is especially important for an ethnomethodologist to come to terms with Fodor's position because important voices within ethnomethodology (e.g., Aaron Cicourel)[3] have endorsed one or another variant of the programme of cognitive psychology and psycholinguistics as a model for emulation, even as a candidate for a theoretical synthesis. Ethnomethodology, these days, orients to diverse theoretical (or, strictly, philosophical) foundations: phenomenology, cognitivism and ordinary-language philosophy (logical grammar). Since I want to assert the relevance – nay, the primacy – of the latter, and since it is in part against this intellectual tradition that Fodor locates his own contribution, there is more at stake in this discussion than the production of a critique for the sake of critique.

Fodor proposes that we must *tolerate* (his term) assumptions such as (i) there are organic processes which can be described as 'computational' in a non-metaphorical sense and (ii) there are sequences of computational 'states' of the nervous system 'causally implicated in the production of behavior'.[4] If we are not prepared to tolerate such assumptions, he claims, then we must 'do without theories in cognitive psychology altogether'.[5] Elsewhere in his book, *The Language of Thought*, he writes: 'the notion of an internal language [= computational medium – JC] is conceptually coherent . . . [and] it is demanded by such cognitive models as sensible people now endorse,'[6] and he eventually asserts that the postulated cognitive processes underlying complex human conduct must be facilitated by fully *discursive* 'representations' in the nervous system (especially in the brain), doubting the 'very intelligibility' of the suggestion that cognitive processes could be carried out in other than a discursive medium.[7] With this, he commits himself to a version of information-processing and transformation in terms of explicitly linguistic-conceptual media *within* the nervous system. Not surprisingly, the reader of these theses is warned by Fodor himself that 'some of the things we seem to be committed to strike me, frankly, as a little wild; I should be glad to know if there are ways of saving the psychology while avoiding those commitments.'[8] He nonetheless seeks to promote discussion on these points,[9] and it is to his credit to have brought out into the open many assumptions and speculative credos tacitly (albeit tenaciously) espoused in cognitive theorising.

The idea of 'saving the psychology' is, I think, ambiguous. If it means saving cognitive theory as it is presently articulated, then I am not sanguine about the prospects. If it means saving the phenomena as worthy of theoretical elucidation, then, in so far as thinking, understanding, recognising, deciding, speaking and engaging in courses of complex activity may be thought of as 'psychological' in some sense, I believe that there are ways to 'save' them for study. The nature of the appropriate domain for their study, however, may not be commensurate with Fodor's overall perspective. But more on that later.

What sort of thing does Fodor have in mind when he speaks of fully discursive internal computational media (his 'language of thought')? The following instance can clarify this: 'deciding', he claims, 'is a computational process: the act the agent performs is the consequence of computations defined over representations of possible actions. No representations, no computations. No computations, no model.'[10] The computations putatively involved in any 'process' of deciding would be of 'a set of hypotheticals of roughly the form, if Bi [a behavioural option – JC] performed in S [a certain situation – JC], then, with a certain probability, Ci [a certain anticipated consequence will ensue – JC].'[11] Since he defines 'deciding' in terms of computations defined over 'representations of possible actions'[12] he must theoretically endow the human central nervous system (and the CNS of higher primates to whom 'deciding' may be ascribed) with 'available means for representing not only its behavioral options but also: the probable consequence of acting on those options, a preference ordering defined over the consequences and, of course, the original situation in which it [the organism – JC] finds itself.'[13] The conceptual richness of the representational machinery is formidable: its complexity and structure is, as Fodor discusses it, tantamount to that of any natural language.

In this example, I think we can find many of the problems which beset Fodor's treatment of human conduct in computational terms. The first of these centres upon the method of the logical regimentation of concepts of conduct. Fodor himself criticises behaviourism for indulging in what he terms 'a prima facie implausible reduction of calculated actions to habit',[14] noting that any scheme which construes conduct as a series of trained *responses* to environmental inputs neglects (amongst other things) the creativity of conduct. Behaviourism, thus, is guilty of a fundamental misconstrual of the logic of relevant predicates of human conduct, oversimplifying their meanings in the interest of a stipulated epistemological commitment (reductionism). However, in treating 'deciding' as he does, Fodor also neglects the complex logical grammar of its use in the language, preferring to regiment its meaning in the interest of neo-mentalistic epistemology. Because '*trying to decide*' can involve human beings in considering (perhaps visualising) some range of possibilities (actions, consequences) in any given situation, we should not think that 'deciding' itself is invariantly the upshot of processes (e.g., deliberations) characteristic of 'trying to decide'. Indeed, it can make perfect sense to say of me that I decided to do something in situations when all that is relevant is that at some point I had expressed doubts about doing it but did, in the end, do it. I need not have engaged in any protracted deliberations nor need I have been engaged in 'trying to decide'. My 'deciding' to do what I did may simply have been expressed in a shrug of the shoulders and a doing of the thing I did after all. In what sense, then, *must* we postulate a 'computational process' as constituting 'deciding'? I am not so much complaining about the obvious idealisation involved in Fodor's description of the sort of deliberations in which one might engage when 'trying to decide', nor, at this point, about the transformation of conscious deliberations into unconscious 'computations'. I am arguing that he is not describing 'deciding' *at all* in any recognisable way. Surely we must be more careful in delineating our subject domain than this, especially if we want to generate theoretical explanations for it. Deciding is not strictly a process or course of action; it is an upshot or terminus or outcome. Locutions such as: 'he spent a long time deciding what he should do on his day off' may appear to make deciding a course of action, but as a linguist Fodor should know that such a locution disguises the logic of the verb involved. In a sentence such as this one, 'deciding' amounts to 'trying (successfully in the end) to decide'.

Elsewhere, Fodor proposes that he is advancing a theory which 'makes understanding a sentence analogous to computational processes whose character we roughly comprehend. On this view, what happens when a person understands a sentence must be a translation process basically analogous to what happens when a machine "understands" (viz., compiles) a sentence in its programming language.'[15] And yet this presupposes that 'understanding' is a temporally extended course of action, an assumption that is quite at odds with the logico-grammatical facts. Understanding is an *achievement*, not a course of action.[16] Whatever may occur in someone's mind or brain when he is trying to understand, or when he is under the (perhaps false) impression that he has understood, is not constitutive of his actual understanding. Further evidence to show how Fodor is wedded to a purely internalist conception of the meaning of 'understanding' is the following passage:

> in general, any behavior whatever is compatible with understanding, or failing to understand, any predicate whatever. Pay me enough and I will stand on my head *iff* you say 'chair'. But I know what 'is a chair' means all the same.[17]

He is here defending a view in which understanding a predicate is a wholly inner *occurrence* rather than a publicly ratifiable achievement, and, on this purely internal account, public conduct becomes epiphenomenal. The problem is that public conduct in appropriate circumstances is exactly what enables us to know of

ourselves and each other that indeed we have understood whatever it is that is at issue. How could I ratify Fodor's avowal that he
understands what 'is a chair' means unless I could appeal to some
specific instances of his situated conduct, especially his illocutionary conduct of using this predicate in well-formed expressions in
appropriate circumstances in spontaneous ways? In his rush to
escape from the restrictiveness of Skinnerian renditions of 'understanding a predicate' in terms of sets of dispositions to respond to
some fixed array of environmental 'stimuli' with that predicate,
Fodor has forgotten that, in the ordinary non-'technical' sense of
'behaviour', it must be by virtue of his behaviour and its contexts
that we can ratify his claim to 'understand' anything whatsoever.

Another example of Fodor's penchant for linguistic over-
simplification when engaged in theorising is his treatment of the
concept of 'thought'. Having successfully argued that thoughts
cannot be reduced to, or analysed without residue into, mental
images, he then asserts: 'For thoughts are the kinds of things that
can be true or false: they are thus the kinds of things that are
expressed by *sentences*, not words.'[18] Indeed, *some* thoughts (i.e.,
propositional ones) can have truth-values, but some cannot. If I
have a sudden thought about the traffic-jam I am likely to
encounter as I drive home, there is no sense in which it is either
true or false, whether the thought is expressed by a mental image
of queues of cars and blaring horns or discursively by some
soliloquistic locution such as, e.g., and *inter alia*, 'Damn that
Storrow Drive exit!' Moreover, some thoughts can, of course, be
expressed in single words (leaving aside the rather obvious objection that sentences are made of words and can hardly be contrasted to them). I might have a thought of my wife and simply
say (silently) her name to myself; I might have a thought about an
overdue library book and express it purely in terms of its one-
word title, and so on.

We have certainly not penetrated to the core of Fodor's theory
in discussing examples such as these. My reason for considering
this series of cases is twofold. Primarily, I think that it is indicative
of Fodor's penchant for unilateral reformulation of ordinary
concepts, a practice which blinds him to their actual logic of use.

Secondly, and derivatively, I believe that it is mainly by indulging in such unilateral redescriptions and reformulations of ordinary concepts and predicates that he can get his theoretical programme off the ground in the first place. It is this issue that I want to address in some detail next. In order to be clear about its pervasiveness for the entire enterprise in which Fodor and others are engaged, we must backtrack a little and consider an early (and foundational) statement by Hilary Putnam, whose speculative work on minds and machines, brains and behaviour,[19] informs a good deal of contemporary cognitivist theory.

When we take a fresh look at Putnam's proposed domain for any psychophysiological explanation of human conduct based upon the computer analogy, it turns out to have been remarkably restrictive:

> In order to avoid 'category mistakes', it is necessary to restrict this notion, 'explain human behavior', very carefully. Suppose a man says 'I feel bad'. His behavior, described in one set of categories, is: 'stating that he feels bad'. And the explanation may be "He said that he felt bad because he was hungry and had a headache". I do not wish to suggest that the event 'Jones *stating* that he feels bad' can be explained in terms of the laws of *physics*. But there is *another* event which is very relevant, namely, 'Jones's body producing such-and-such sound waves.' . . . it is the sense in which these are the 'same event' . . . that is relevant here.[20]

Putnam goes on to propose that what *he* means when he speaks of 'causally explaining human behavior' is causally explaining certain physical events (motions of bodies, emissions of sound waves, etc.) which, he claims, are the *same* as the events which make up human *behaviour*. He adds, testily, that 'no amount of Ryle-ism' can succeed in arguing away that physical/neurophysiological science might explain that much.[21] In like manner, Fodor, in an earlier work,[22] proposes that 'it would be a sufficient condition for the causal explanation of an action' that such an action might be analysed as a *motion* performed by an organism (or person) in a certain state (presumably of its CNS), and that sufficient causal conditions can be formulated for being in that state, e.g., in physiological terms. (We shall return to some additional problems with this argument further on.)

What are we to make of claims such as these, claims upon which much of the theoretical edifice of the computational approach to conduct appears to depend? Let us return to Putnam's argument that there is a sense in which the event 'Jones stating that he feels bad' and the event 'Jones's body producing such-and-such sound waves' are identical. Although one can perfectly well say that in stating anything one is producing sound waves, the pronoun 'one' here cannot be understood purely in terms of 'one's body', but must be understood in terms of 'one' as a *person*. To say of Jones that it was his *body* which was producing sound waves (of whatever acoustic shape or wave frequency) strongly and ineliminably presupposes that at the time of this event Jones himself (the *person*) was not controlling his speech himself, that it was an involuntary emission from his body, produced indeed by factors endogenous *to* the body but not produced by Jones, *qua* speaker. Moreover, there is a serious equivocality being exploited in all this which rests upon our interpretation of the concept of 'behaviour'. If 'behaviour' is to mean 'bodily occurrences or happenings' (e.g., motions, sound wave emissions, etc.), then I think we are being seriously misled. Even if we are prepared to treat organic occurrences and emissions (movements and sounds) as 'behavioural events' (and I do not really see why we *should* do this), these are certainly not the events which make up *human* behaviour. *Human* behaviour is made up of activities (including stating things) *whose ascription conditions are logically irreducible to those for organic occurrences and emissions.* Behaviouristic doctrines notwithstanding, the concept of 'human behaviour' simply does not, in its logical grammar of rational use, encompass such phenomena. In various locutions such as 'the behaviour of his endocrine glands is causing us concern', we are, of course, not referring to *human* behaviour but to the behaviour of glands. That there are non-humans which 'behave' (including parts of humans) is no argument in favour of reductionism in the case of 'human behaviour'.

Let us suppose, however, that we had properly identified some phenomenon as a body producing sound waves of a certain sort, or a body moving in a certain fashion. I think that we would be likely to *cancel* this description of the phenomenon if it turned out that it was, in fact, a person saying something or doing something. (At least if we started out with no theoretical axe to grind). I want to distinguish this position from a closely related but, I believe, subsidiary one. Bernard Harrison, for example, states:

> The accumulation of information about a series of bodily movements *never*, in itself, serves to make it any more probable that a particular action word applies to the person [*not* his body – JC] who is executing those movements, for a description of bodily movements is invariably compatible with more than one description in terms of actions.[23]

Thus, a description of me in terms of waving my hand is fully compatible with a description of me in terms of, *inter alia*, greeting a friend, wafting away a fly, signalling someone to stop, etc. However, this is a description of *me*, and of *my* waving *my* hand: we are still at the *person* level. It is I who am moving (a part of) my body, not my body that is moving *simpliciter*. Contrary to Putnam and Fodor, any action-description formulated with 'my (his, her, your) body' in subject position (e.g., 'my body was producing too much adrenalin') removes the person from consideration and must be restricted to events which are simply not coextensive with predicates of personal conduct as such. One can describe a person as executing bodily movements, but not his *body* as executing bodily movements unless one is describing involuntary organic episodes. Since 'stating that he feels bad' is not an involuntary organic episode taking place in Jones's body, it is quite erroneous to stipulate that Jones's action is the same thing as his body's producing such-and-such sound waves, even though in stating what he did *Jones* produced sound waves. Strawson was surely correct to identify the concept of 'person' as a 'primitive' in our language, especially in our language of conduct.[24]

It is crucial to distinguish in this connection between what

J. F. M. Hunter has called 'a plain neurological explanation' of how we talk (etc.)[25] and the sort of psychophysiological programme which Putnam and Fodor have in mind. After all, no-one wants to deny the obvious fact that our central nervous system processes have something to do with our speaking. The issue is: what is this 'something to do with' supposed to cover? It is known, for example, that electrochemical impulses emanating from parts of the cortex are transmitted along nerve fibres to the laryngeal and circumoral components of the physiological apparatus for speech, among other CNS events. But what could all this have to do with a description such as 'encoding a message in words' or 'decoding' one? Hunter remarks pertinently that any process which we isolated in the cortex could scarcely be a neurological instantiation of 'encoding' or of 'arriving at what we shall say' except by an arbitrary anthropomorphism: we have regular ascription criteria for saying of someone that they are engaged in a process of 'encoding' or 'decoding' messages (a Morse code operator, say, amongst a variety of conceivable possibilities), whereas we have absolutely no criteria whatsoever for predicating such a complex operation of the cortex. Moreover, we have no clear conception about what could be meant by encoding something into *words* unless the original was not itself available in symbols, and it is difficult (to say the least) to conceive of something called a 'message' forming in the cortex. (Of course, we say metaphorically of nerve impulses that they convey 'messages' to and from the cortex, but *these* sorts of 'messages' are hardly the kinds of phenomena which could be cited in any account of a 'thing we seek to communicate, articulate, put into words, speak or say'.)

> I cannot see what reasons we would have for saying that any process that we isolated [in the CNS – JC] was the process of 'arriving at what we say', or of anything else if, *ex hypothesi*, it was not shown to be correlated with a process, *otherwise discernible*, which could be described as, for example, 'arriving at what we say'. [my italics][26]

Hunter notes that the ascription criteria for ascribing such a predicate as 'arriving at what (I, we, they, you, etc.) say' would be context-bound and occasioned rather than invariantly applicable to a speaker, and he adds:

> I find it impossible to conjecture what explanatory force such a discovery [of a neural process accompanying an instance of arriving at what one said – JC] would have. (It is not like being puzzled as to how someone does something apparently very difficult, and then being shown his system, and finding it easy after all.) It would show that we do have certain physical equipment for doing it [i.e., speaking creatively – JC]; *but whether that is the case was never part of the problem.*[27]

It does seem to me that the sort of *psycho*physiological programme which Putnam had in mind would require *more than* the sort of neurophysiological description (however empirically elaborated in the language of neurophysiology, biochemistry etc.) just outlined in schematic form. This does not satisfy Fodor, who argues for a model of the speaker-hearer along the following lines:

> A speaker is a mapping from messages onto wave forms, and a hearer is a mapping from wave forms onto messages. . . . The speaker, in short, has a value of M [message – JC] in mind and the hearer can tell which value of M it is.[28]

Further, Fodor hypothesises that:

> 1. The mapping from messages to wave forms and vice versa is indirect: Wave forms are paired with messages via the computation of a number of intervening representations.
> 2. Among these intervening representations there are several which correspond to the structural descriptions of sentences which generative grammars provide.[29]

The CNS is now burdened with 'encoding/decoding to and from wave forms'[30] and 'computing the structural description of those sentences which express that message'.[31] Now, in the article by Putnam from which I have been quoting, it is claimed that 'the functional organization (problem-solving, thinking) of the human being or machine can be described in terms of sequences of mental or logical states respectively (and the accompanying verbalisations) without reference to the nature of the 'physical realization' of these states'.[32] In this light, we can begin to understand the choice of theoretical vocabulary by Fodor: more than a 'plain neurological account' is held out as a real requirement by Putnam,[33] and by Fodor himself in his early work, such that speaking and hearing are to be construed *literally* as CNS encoding and decoding of 'wave forms' to and from 'messages'.[34] That a Gricean semantics is at work in Fodor's own version of this mentalistic position is clear: 'a speaker is, above all, someone with something to communicate. For want of a better term, I shall call what he has in mind a message'.[35] This translates Grice's intentionalist theory of communicative under- standing, according to which a hearer must invariantly be involved in grasping the speaker's intentions informing his utterances, into a part of his computational-cognitive theory.

I think we can best begin to untangle these claims by noting that none of the postulated 'messages', 'encodings and decod- ings', and 'computations' of 'intervening representations' – the 'sequences of mental states', to return to Putnam – are known by or to the speaker-hearer. They are all posited as *unconscious*, as phenomena occurring *within* the cortex and CNS. But we are not given any criteria by which to pick out their CNS realisations, or manifestations. A theory such as this, then, effectively says nothing to empirical neuroscientific research. And how could it? It begins by *redescribing* what it is that speakers can hear so as to render unitary all their objects of hearing and listening; they hear 'wave forms'. (Elsewhere, Fodor states that the fundamental question for the computational theory of communications is: how can speaker-hearers communicate by 'the production of acoustic wave forms?'[36]) Having rendered everything heard and listened to by human beings devoid of meaning by stipulation, and *ab initio*, it is necessary then to find some way of 'adding the mean- ing' to the sound waves. The 'mind' is the candidate for the agent of message detection, only in so far as it does this *un-consciously* (since we are not conscious of continuously adding meanings to noises we pick up and *thence* finding them to have been meaningful utterances). Note how this formulation of what people do when they speak and understand each other echoes Putnam's behaviouristic reduction of a predicate like 'stating' into one as denuded and impoverished as 'producing sound waves of such-and-such frequency'. No wonder Fodor (and, tacitly, Putnam) posit complex internal computational and encoding/decoding operations to account for the possibility of our speaking, hearing and understanding meaningful utterances in our everyday life: they deny that we ever hear an utterance, and claim that all we ever *really* hear are 'sound waves' or 'wave forms'. Now, this logically precludes our preserving any distinc-tion in ordinary language between 'hearing a noise', 'hearing a sound' (or 'mere sound'), 'picking up an acoustic signal' and actually *hearing someone say something that made sense as an utterance in the talk*. In fact, Fodor (and Putnam) can only get their cognitive-mentalist (or 'unconscious computational') metatheory off the ground by denying a plain fact of human experience: that we can directly hear utterances *without* averting to something we have *in mind*. The denial of this plain truism leads to the postulation of something lurking in the *unconscious* mind to take the place of the mental 'message' or 'meaning' (of which we are not aware) as an addendum to having heard someone produce a noise. It simply makes no sense to argue that we are constantly engaged in an activity, viz., finding the right message corresponding to a heard sound ('wave form'), adding it and realising that it is an *utterance*, or a string of *words*, that mean such-and-such. So, in order to *invent* a phenomenon for elucidation, we have a mythical process (at best a description of a translator or decipherer of codes translating off a tape-recording of sounds that turn out to be words and utterances in a foreign language) turned into a quite superfluous *central-nervous-system* function! It is as if I always needed a book of face-photographs to consult before I could ever recognise anyone from day to day and, given that I have no such book, its equivalent is stored away inside me for consultation by other parts of my insides, all out of my awareness (or even interest!) so as to enable me to recognise things. (A theory based upon just such a way of thinking is called a 'projective pattern-recognition theory', whether it be of the 'template-matching' or 'feature-extraction' or some other variety.) We have yet to locate the grounds for taking *any* such theory seriously.

If we hear something which we do *not* understand, we might seek some code by means of which to decipher or render intelligible the sequence of sounds or words. This is an *occasioned* practice in which human beings (and only human beings and certain advanced computational artefacts) engage.

Our understanding of human conduct is not advanced by positing theoretical fictions such as *mental* operations of which we are supposed *not* to be conscious, whose location would have to be the cortex or CNS, and yet whose description is based entirely upon the use of activity-predicates and thereby *upon public procedures* of which we *are* fully conscious when ascribably engaged in them: e.g., 'arriving at what we shall say', 'encoding/decoding messages', 'analysing', 'computing', 'having something in mind and mulling it over', etc. (There is a good deal of slippage in the selection of terms; 'mental' can become equivalent to 'cortical' or 'CNS-based' in some passages and 'conscious', 'software', 'programme-based' in other usages by Fodor.)

Consider the range of Fodor's actual extension of our ordinary concepts of mental states and processes. In ordinary parlance, mental *states* would be thought of as including, *inter alia*, being depressed, being in pain, concentrating, being 'high', hypnotised, agitated, grief-stricken, etc. Mental *processes* might include: calculating in the head, silent soliloquies of various kinds, visualising, picturing or imag(in)ing some scene to oneself, or daydreaming. Mental *operations* could include the sorts of things listed here as mental processes, and other ones in addition. Mental *events* might include such mundanely known-about and conscious events as a stabbing pain suddenly distracting one, or a thought suddenly striking one. Yet it is clear from Fodor's usage that he means *none* of these commonplace things when he postulates that whatever an organism (including a person) does is determined 'by its mental states, processes, events, operations and so forth'[37] along with 'specified features of its environment.'[38] Indeed, the sort of things which Fodor postulates as 'complex mental operations'[39] appear to be largely *unconscious*, such as the so-called 'unconscious inferences and other paramechanical transactions'[40] supposedly necessitated by an explanation of perceptual constancy, among other phenomena. I am, for example, thought to have mental operations involved in applying a *recipe*[41] to a melody-line in order to recognise it under sensory transformations of restricted types as one and the same melody or tune. And since I can recognise *Lillibullero* when it is played as a waltz, on a warped record, played as a march etc., I do not know nor apply any *recipe* nor experience characteristic mental operations of any sort, then all of this is predicated not of *me* but of my nervous system functioning, and is utterly without appropriate ascription conditions! Using or applying recipes is something available as a type of conduct only to human beings as whole persons or certain advanced computational artefacts designed to simulate such human actions, *not* human brains or CNS's. A computational artefact which could be said to be literally applying a recipe to anything whatever would have to fulfil *public* ascription criteria, such as displaying the results of doing what it is programmed to do, viz. using its program to compute the answers . . . . It makes no sense to predicate of nervous systems the using or applying of recipes (propositional rules, codes, etc.) except as a wholly unexplicated metaphor of some sort. This formulation of perceptual constancy begs more questions than the initial phenomenon it is designed to explain.[42]

2 ON FODOR'S PSYCHOPHYSIOLOGICAL DETERMINISM

In *The Language of Thought*, we read:

> When we think of an organism as a computer, we attempt to assign formulae in the vocabulary of a psychological theory to physical states of the organism (e.g., to states of its nervous

system). Ideally, the assignment should be carried through in such a fashion that (some, at least) of the sequences of states that are causally implicated in the production of behavior can be interpreted as computations which have appropriate descriptions of the behavior as their 'last line'. . . . In short, the organic events which we accept as implicated in the etiology of behavior will turn out to have two theoretically relevant descriptions.[19]

One such description will be physical and lawlike, the other will be 'psychological' and thus, for Fodor, 'computational'. Moreover, Fodor asserts that the rules for the computations are themselves represented somehow in the nervous system so that '*a representation of the rules they follow constitutes one of the causal determinants of their* [organisms' – JC] *behavior.*'[44]

I want to claim that such a theory is essentially a 'computerese' translation of a familiar metaphysical theme, viz., that whatever I do is the *invariant* outcome or product of prior ratiocination, calculation, discursive reasoning, etc., *whether I am aware of it or not.* And since if I am not even aware of constantly being engaged in antecedent activities such as 'analysing', and could not avow the steps I am supposed to be computing prior to engaging in the myriad of spontaneous but meaningful things I do, then it is just asserted that it is not *I as a person* who is doing these things, but parts of my insides (cortex, CNS). Amidst the micro-processes of neuronal discharges and synaptic transmissions there are not only computations of 'appropriate descriptions of the behavior'[45] in which I am engaged, (with no attention paid to the vexing question of who or what is supposed to 'read' or 'use' such 'descriptions' and why), but there are also, wired in, so to speak, cortical encodings of the 'rules' governing the computational routines that are supposed to eventuate in or 'determine' (in part) my behaviour (what it is I say or do). Note that it is *my brain* that is following these rules, and not me as a person, contrary to what is implied in the expression 'a representation of the rules they follow' where 'they' refers not to brains but to whole 'organisms' including human beings.

J. F. M. Hunter, in his now classic rebuttal of the Chomsky – Katz mentalistic theory of linguistic creativity,[46] had this to say of such a model:

> [In] the case of talking, it is just the lack of evidence that in the ordinary sense we operate a system of rules that leads us to posit microprocesses. We lack precisely the evidence we need to establish that rule-following is going on in the nervous system.[47]

Indeed, 'not only can we not establish whether a microprocess is the counterpart of a conscious process when the latter does not occur', it is barely intelligible to propose that a nervous system should remember and apply rules governing what to say and how to say it.[48] And how does Fodor suppose that any rules relating to linguistic communication become encoded in the nervous system (including the cortex)?

He grasps this nettle by claiming, after Chomsky, that we do indeed acquire a set of truth-rules governing the extension of predicates whilst children, as we are learning to speak properly in our first natural language. These rules which we, or rather, our brains, acquire, are supposed to facilitate the internal computations mapping those mysterious internal 'messages' onto waveforms which activate the appropriate neurological equipment embodying the computational resources. To this line of argument, Malcolm has raised a variety of cogent objections. He writes:

> [According to Fodor] all concept learning, all perceptual recognition, all purposeful behavior, *requires* the forming, testing and confirming of generalizations. For example, no one has mastered the English predicate 'is a building' unless he has learned that it falls under a generalization of this form: 'y is a building' is true if and only if Gx. . . . This [logicist – JC] assumption is in conflict with Wittgenstein's insight into the notion of 'family resemblances'. Fodor has read Wittgenstein but has failed to grasp this point. Apparently he has confused it with the

fact that many predicates of ordinary language are 'fuzzy-edged', i.e., in some cases have no determinate truth-value. This is an important point, but it is not what 'family resemblance' means. To say that the word 'game' ranges over a 'family of cases' means that there is *nothing* common to all games on account of which we call all of them games. It does *not* mean that there is something common to all games, namely, a family resemblance . . . . Whenever a word is a family resemblance word *there is no true generalization* that determines its extension – unless one allows as a 'generalization' the triviality that '*x* is a building' is true if and only if *x* is a building. If there is no generalization determining the extension of a predicate there is no 'truth rule' for that predicate.[49]

In so far as this line of argument is correct, and I believe that it is, then Fodor has no theoretical need to posit truth-rules as part of some set of propositional rules (grammars) which the child supposedly somehow *internalises directly into its nervous system*. Since of course children can and do learn to speak their first natural language without having to engage (*per impossibile*) in the complexities of grammatical analysis and truth-rule induction, it is too often then asserted by psycholinguists and others in the cognitive tradition following Chomsky that their *brains* must be doing the complex grammatical analysis and rule-induction. The computational twist on the 'intellectualist legend' against which Ryle argued so effectively thirty years ago is beginning to appear not only conceptually troublesome but perhaps wholly un-necessary for at least some of the factual domains to which it has been addressed as a candidate explanation.

It is a fundamental feature of the computational theory of conduct outlined by Fodor and others,[50] that it must intellectual-ise mundane achievements on the part of persons whose capacities to engage in them have been acquired without anything remotely resembling propositional instruction in terms of rules, decision-procedures and computational algorithms and routines. Depict-ing the acquisition of natural-language competence in terms of the literal 'internalisation' of some set of rules is just as idle as depicting a child's capacity to add numbers together, once acquired, as facilitated by his having *also* learned (mysteriously) the principle of the commutativity of addition or Peano's axioms. When children learn to count and to add, they do not extrapolate and store *any* such discursive information (for who presents it to them and how could they understand, remember and use it at that stage of development were it even consciously accessible to them?). Children are not baby scientists or theoretical linguists/logicians/mathematicians, making and testing hypotheses and working out formal analytic rules for what they hear, see, say and do, even though their successful achievements in adding, counting and speaking *may accord with* the propositionally statable prescriptions of Peano's axioms or generative-grammatical syntax rules. Confusing the fact of being *in accord with a rule* with the fact of being *guided by a known rule*, Fodor, Chomsky, Katz, and others are all led to the postulation of their diverse versions of cognitivist computationism. We would do well to bear in mind that when I learn to corner on a bicycle I need neither know nor apply any complex ergonomic principle (such as the one Polanyi states: a cyclist must keep his balance by adjusting the curvature of his forward path in proportion to the ratio of his unbalance over the square of his speed),[51] and the same holds for other modes of conduct. In fact, a major issue in theoretical linguistics and in ethnomethodological studies is the recognition (expressed also by Anderson in our original quotation) that any form of conduct may be subsumed under a diverse and indefinite set of extensionally equivalent rules. As Baker and Hacker observe:

> The notion of tacit knowledge is neither unknown nor in principle illegitimate, although it needs to be explained and its limits circumscribed. Nevertheless, there must, in this case, be something that will reveal the difference between tacit knowledge of these rules and ignorance of them, something *other* than the mere fact of the speaker's correct discourse. If his correct discourse is *all* that shows his tacit knowledge . . . then the hypothesis that he can produce and understand new sentences because of such tacit knowledge is both untestable

and vacuous, and the very claim that he possesses tacit knowledge is empty. The mere (theoretic) possibility of concocting
a set of rules the product of whose application coincides with a
fragment of our speech does not show that we tacitly know
these rules.[52]

I have discussed various aspects of this part of the argument
elsewhere. I find the case conclusive, but its proponents appear so
tightly wedded to an inner-mechanism theory that we may well be
witnessing a real incommensurability arising in the non-biological
human sciences on this most fundamental point.

The student of these matters may find excellent overviews of
what has been *achieved* in the programming of computers to produce
grammatical sentences in a natural language from a variety of
sources.[53] I do not propose to enter into the details of Winograd's
SHRDLU, of Anderson's ACT, Weizenbaum's ELIZA or
Bobrow's STUDENT,[54] all of them enormously impressive
technical achievements in their own right, but having little or no
bearing on either the study of the neurological phenomena facilitating human speech and comprehension nor on the epistemological
questions here at issue. I am not developing a critique of artificial-
intelligence research and technology – far from it, even though
absurdly inflated claims were once made for its relevance to understanding human 'cognitive processes' at the *unconscious* level. The
abandonment of the view that there are any such phenomena to be
simulated, at least in the ways in which Fodor and others describe
them, leaves all the exciting and brilliant work in AI quite un-
scathed. In so far as AI is self-understood to be concerned with
constructing devices that can mechanically perform complex tasks
rapidly and efficiently, with increasingly sophisticated tasks being
added to the existing repertoire (such as chess-playing), I do not
think that it need be assessed *at all* in connection with psychophysiological meta-theory, any more than progress in advanced
cartography needs to be assessed in terms of the needs of theorising
about children's (or non-technical adults') map-using capacities.

I want to conclude this section with some relevant reminders
from Weizenbaum:

Our ignorance of brain function is currently so very nearly total that we could not even begin to frame appropriate research strategies . . . . A microanalysis of brain functions is, moreover, no more useful for understanding anything about thinking than a corresponding analysis of the pulses flowing through a computer would be for understanding what program the computer is running. Such analyses would simply be at the wrong conceptual level.[55]

My nervous system *enables* me to speak, to say what I say and do what I do, but it is *I*, not my brain, that does these things. This is a fundamental logico-grammatical point, not a point about some mysterious inner function named by the word 'I'. The conduct in which I engage cannot be described purely in terms of the series of organic transformations involved in its production; whereas I smile, my nervous system works to affect my circumoral muscles.

3 'SUB-PERSONAL' INFORMATION-PROCESSING AND THE PERSON

One friendly critic of Fodor's approach, D. C. Dennett, raises a number of issues in connection with the whole project of specifying *cognitive* 'states and processes' thought to 'underlie' various sorts of activities in which human beings can engage. In addressing himself to the claim of Fodor's that discursive rules of conduct are physiologically represented in nervous systems, Dennett has this to say:

(S)uppose hamsters are interpretable as good Bayesians when it comes to the decisions they make. Must we in principle be able to find some saliencies in the hamsters' controls that are interpretable as tokens of formulae in some Bayesian calculus?[56]

Dennett argues that such a proposal is as misplaced as one

which would insist on positing some explicit tokening (embodiment, realisation) of some chess-playing strategy inside a chess-playing computer. He notes that, 'for all the many levels of explicit representation to be found in that [chess-playing – JC] program, nowhere is anything roughly synonymous with "I should get my queen out early" explicitly tokened.'[57] As he goes on to argue, such a (legitimate) way of describing the strategy of a chess-playing computer is an 'emergent property' of computational processes with 'engineering reality', not a description of some component of the actual media by which the computations are effected.

In this way, Dennett affirms his own rather distinctive approach to theory-construction in cognitive science:

> If one agrees with Fodor that it is the job of cognitive psychology to map the psychologically real processes in people, then since the ascription of belief and desire is only indirectly tied to such processes, one might well say that beliefs and desires are not the proper objects of study of cognitive psychology. Put otherwise, cognitivist theories are or should be theories of the subpersonal level, where beliefs and desires disappear, to be replaced with representations of other sorts on other topics.[58]

Given the reticence Dennett exhibits about assigning discursive representations of certain sorts to nervous systems, and his disclaimer on the *theoretical* relevance of person-level predicates such as 'believes' and 'desires', the stage is set for a thorough-going change of levels of analysis and speculation. For Dennett, a mature cognitive science must *dispense with* (most of) our ordinary, vernacular mental predicates. Because our pre-theoretical vocabulary for speaking about 'the mental' fails to 'pick out' natural kinds of psychological domains susceptible to connections with the nervous system and its putative computational 'states', Dennett complains about the 'conceptual infelicities and incoherencies of various sorts' characteristic of – 'embodied' in – our ordinary mental language.[59] Elsewhere, he refers to 'our everyday attributions in mentalistic or intentional language' as something of 'a mess', as compared, say, to Turing-machine talk.[60] And here Dennett begins his move to the level of the 'sub-personal' in his search for natural kinds of perspicuous reference usable in cognitive theorising.

Dennett's view of the nature of our vernacular mental concepts and predicates implicitly treats them as *embodying a theory of the mind*, as (essentially defective) theoretical constructs. He bemoans the fact that 'beliefs' and 'pains', and states of 'being in pain' (etc.) do not label definable *things* or states. As theoretical attributes [61] – to use his term – these concepts and predicates are simply not 'well-behaved'.[62]

The counter-argument begins here, for Dennett has no good argument in favour of treating ordinary mental concepts and predicates as *theoretical* concepts, susceptible to assessment in terms of standards of *theory*-construction in some scientific endeavour. To so assess them would be tantamount to judging a move in chess according to the rules of poker. Why should anyone insist that, because the concept of 'believe' is unusable for labelling some neatly discriminable object in the world (or fixed extension of objects), to that extent it is *defective*? The logic of a concept like 'believe' is such as to preclude the relevance to its analytic explication of standards like these. Indeed, since Dennett no-where attempts to reconcile his account of the ordinary meanings of these concepts with any rival conceptual elucidation available in the literature of analytical and ordinary-language philosophy, he is spared the problem of having to defend his treatment of them as intrinsically defective theoretical-entity terms. We are given no *criteria* according to which our normal mental talk is 'conceptually incoherent', intrinsically 'a mess', and so forth. Perhaps this is because were Dennett to have made the effort to *specify* such criteria, he would have rapidly encountered the fact that, whilst *some* of our uses of our ordinary mental language in avowals, ascriptions, ratifications and negations, may be found in some contexts and for some purposes to be 'incoherent', messy, unclear, imprecise, etc., it should be remembered that these judgements would only be logically available against a background of criteria for adequate, precise, clear, justified uses-in-context. There are no generic, decontextualised criteria for saying of everything we do with the use of our ordinary mental language-domain that it is intrinsically *hypothetical* or *theoretical* and also *defectively* so. Such claims do not even belong in this region of our language/speech.

We are none of us committed to any theory of the mind just in so far as we use our mental language properly in everyday life, any more than we are committed to, say, the bile theory of the humours when we say of someone that he is 'melancholic' or to a biblical-supernatural conception of miracles when we say of someone that 'his escape was a miracle'. I have neither a defective nor a coherent *theory* of 'belief', of mind, of you, just in so far as I can say of you that you believe that X, or in X, or something about X, etc. My ascriptions are not assessable in terms of considerations having to do with an hypostatisation of mind in theoretical schemes, but on practical, normative and contextual grounds alone. (And therein lies a logic unto itself awaiting fuller elucidation.)

Dennett's move to the 'sub-personal' level may appear at first simply to be a move to doing pure neurophysiology. In *this* domain, the relevant concept of 'information' is neither propositional, linguistic, discursive nor sentential. It is more likely to be understood in terms of *physical* parameters such as constellations of neuronal inputs and outputs, the modification of neuronal signals, the transformation of the activity vectors of brain cells, in which 'information processing' becomes a largely mechanistic affair.[63] Cognate notions of 'information' derive from the mathematical information theory of Shannon and Weaver[64] or the statistical theory of thermodynamics where 'information' refers simply to negative entropy.[65] There is nothing in such a conception to suggest that descriptions of neural activity in terms of information processing may be mapped onto the sort of discursive renditions advanced by Fodor, Chomsky and others in their tradition in other than a wholly arbitrary manner. How, then, does Dennett hope to connect his 'sub-personal' domain of CNS states and processes with the 'personal' level of 'intentional-system' or 'mental' discourse to warrant a claim for 'cognitive' science?

Dennett's answer is that we adopt what he calls a 'top-down' strategy. For this, we need to work in artificial-intelligence computer programming and hardware technology, rather than neurophysiology. He writes:

> The task of psychology is to explain human perception, learning, cognition and so forth in terms that will ultimately unite psychological theory to physiology in one way or another . . . a 'top-down' strategy (. . .) begins with a more abstract decomposition of the highest levels of psychological organisation, and hopes to analyze these into more and more detailed smaller systems or processes until finally one arrives at elements familiar to the biologists.[66]

In the service of such a programme, Dennett argues: 'the ultimate millennial goal of AI (artificial intelligence research) must be to provide a hierarchical breakdown of parts in the computer that will mirror or be isomorphic to some hard-to-discover hierarchical breakdown of brain-event parts.'[67] Millennial indeed! Especially when one takes seriously such recent pronouncements on the relevance of computer science to neurophysiological inquiry as the following:

> (Computer) analogies are not wrong in the sense of making false predictions about behavior: they are simply irrelevant, the real brain has a different organisation; the logical structure is different.[68]

Weiskrantz is not alone in this verdict; Granit also demurs from the claims often made about the relevance of computational analogies, even though he acknowledges some conceptual indebtedness to cybernetic thinking. For both Weiskrantz and Granit, the computer analogy is a source of 'elegant irrelevancies'.[69] Of course, some neurophysiologists do articulate their findings employing metaphors taken from computer science. Michael Arbib (who is both a brain scientist and a computer scientist) not surprisingly interprets the findings of the classic neurophysiological study on the visual system of the frog[70] in terms of the frog's retina carrying out 'computations on the visual image'.[71] And the original researchers themselves wrote with considerable stylistic ornamentation about the frog's eye which 'speaks to the brain in a language already highly organized and interpreted, instead of transmitting some more or less accurate copy of the distribution of light on the receptors'.[72] This is clearly an analogical extension of intentional idioms; what their researches showed (according to their own, unelaborated rendition) was that there are pulses conveyed from retinal ganglion cells to layers of terminal cells in the optic tectum of the frog's brain such that the heaviest firing is correlated with four (controllable) qualitative perceptual features in the frog's visual space: (i) boundaries (ii) moving contours (iii) changing contrasts (iv) local dimming. The researchers hypothesise about the existence of 'convexity-sensitive neurons' in terms of an evolutionary function: since the insects which frogs eat may be detected by such a specialised neural apparatus as described, that apparatus can be thought of in innocently teleological terms as a system for 'insect-detection', although of course there is no claim that the information received by the frog's brain from the frog's visual system is in the form of, or interpretable by the frog into, propositional-conceptual information about 'insects'. We need not suppose that *any* kind of information transmitted in this way can be accorded an epistemic description even in humans – and yet this is the level at which neurophysiology operates with the concept of information and its transmission and transformation.

Dennett is no more a neurophysiologist than I am, yet he does not discuss much neurophysiological work in connection with his remarkable claim about the 'isomorphism down to the neuronal level'[73] to be expected from strong AI researches, at least in principle. Nonetheless, he believes, without much supporting argument or documentation, that manufactured computer hardware should be studied intensively so as to furnish the basis for describing the 'hard-to-discover hierarchical breakdown of brain-event parts' in the absence of our having any *independent* criteria for counting something *as* a brain-event part relevant to such an isomorphism. His 'sub-personal' story turns out to be a device for upholding the prospect of a wholly mechanistic understanding of human conduct based solely upon the development of non-human artefacts, and *their* study.

Indeed, Dennett is quite explicit about the 'solution' to Hume's Problem supposedly entailed by a proper consideration of computer functioning. Hume's Problem, as Dennett carefully discusses it, can be formulated in terms of an apparent paradox: given that something is a representation only *for* or *to* someone, how can internal representations (*cf*. Hume's 'impressions' and 'ideas') of the external world enable us (persons) to perceive the external world of which we have such representations? A regress threatens: we have an infinite series of neurological eyes scanning neurological representations with attendant analysers interpreting what they scan. Faced with the absurdity of such a view, we must, argues Dennett, look to 'data structures' in computer science as examples of 'self-understanding representations', noting that it would be mere 'lexicographical purism'[74] to insist that such a metaphorical notion fails to shed light on Hume's Problem. I think that this *is* essentially to play around with the notion of a 'representation'. No-one seriously proposes that a computer programmed with the most advanced conceivable pattern-recognition program is *thereby* endowed with a capacity for having visual experiences, no matter how often we may, *for purposes of convenience or innocent anthropomorphism*, employ such an expression in dealings with it. I hasten to add that for my part I have no idea at all how one might go about explaining how one's nervous system functions enable one to have visual (or any other, e.g., painful) experiences, and I am not even convinced that the question itself is fully coherent if it aims for an answer in terms of the design or physical parameters of the enabling systems. However, I see no valid reason advanced to give up on the very notions of human experience.

Elsewhere, I have discussed Dennett's eliminative-materialist moves against the notion that persons have mental images on occasion.[76] It is significant that images have proved such a problem for his overall materialistic-physicalistic approach; he is prepared to give up on the computer analogy when it comes to dealing with pain, and in his chapter, 'Why You Can't Make a Computer that Feels Pain',[76] he even proposes that neurophysiological work on the Melzack-Wall hypotheses about A-fibres and C-fibres (among other contributions from physiology) would lead one to assert that 'What must be impeached is our ordinary concept of pain'.[77] One wonders how anyone could proceed to study matters relevant to pain if they were to abandon the concept itself, but here again Dennett is erroneously treating 'pain', like 'mental image' and other ordinary mental concepts and predicates as if they were (defective) theoretical hypotheses rather than elements of our fundamental intelligibility system. Science is answerable to extra-scientific reason at least for its coherence.

Various commentators in the sceptical camp have advanced arguments against the view that computational artefacts could (in the logical-possibility sense) be accorded what Searle has called 'intrinsic intentionality'[78] or what Baker has called a 'first-person perspective'.[79] There is always the danger in mounting such principled arguments: critical of AI, Dreyfus, a phenomenological philosopher, was beaten in a game played by a computer programmed with Greenblatt's heuristic plausible-moves generator in 1967.[80] And yet, in view of the current pervasiveness of the computational theory of complex behaviour in the human sciences, it is urgent to clarify the logical space of this doctrine without judging in advance what technology may deliver and what it may not. The problem with the proponents of the computational approach to cognition is not their blind faith in technological progress, but their conviction that such progress in computer science alone illuminates the domain of the mental and the material in the study of *man*.

4 CONCLUSION

In the space of this discussion, I do not see myself as having done any more than expose for critical inspection a series of significant conceptual difficulties in some well-known (and quite widely accepted) statements of the computational-cognitive approach to the study of human conduct. Some of my arguments have been developed from previously-taken positions,[81] and others are more tentative than decisive. However, I maintain that they are sufficiently troublesome to warrant a fresh perspective on a range of topics frequently subsumed exclusively under the domain of this (ruling) paradigm.

At the risk of appearing to sound like a theoretical nihilist to those who see the possibilities in dichotomies, I am neither a behaviourist nor a mentalist, neither a reductionistic materialist nor a metaphysical dualist, and neither a mechanist nor a cognitivist. Yet this is far from rejecting everything offered to us by such doctrines at work. Indeed, nothing could be advanced at all were it not for rival approaches to confront each other with arguments and evidence – although on the latter score, so many experimental researches conducted in non-biological human science strike me as too theory-laden and assumptive in their very *description* to be independent courts of appeal. I have in mind experiments such as those conducted by psycholinguists involving people in converting sentences from active to passive, and the reverse, so as to 'show' something about their 'using' levels of 'deep structure' (where? inside them) and performing 'unconscious' transformational-grammatical derivations into 'surface' utterances.

I would like to conclude on a more positive note by proposing, via two examples of 'problems' formulated and confronted by cognitive scientists, why I am content to settle for common sense rationality in *those* cases. Lest I be radically misunderstood on this, let me again stress that my own understanding of a scientific research programme in the study of cognition would *not* settle for problem-formulations which yield only to dissipation by reference to commonsense rationality. But discussion of my own research is not appropriate at this juncture.

Hunter articulates a beautiful insight of Wittgenstein's in a presentation of Wittgenstein's anti-reductionist view of various human activities, even the most 'organic':

Language use may be said to be an organic process, but the interesting thing to us about organic processes is that *they work*, and hence to us they are *simple*. To describe what goes on in me when I wiggle my toes is not to further explain *how I wiggle them*, what I do in order to bring it about that they wiggle. *That* cannot be further explained. I just wiggle them.[82]

There is, primarily, a distinction to be drawn between 'my wiggling my toes' and 'my toes happening to wiggle' (if one may use the verb 'wiggle' intransitively to denote a mere occurrence or happening). Asked, why did my toes wiggle, I might advert to an internal physiological or external sensory-stimulus determinant. Asked, why did *I* wiggle my toes, no amount of physiological data can in principle be relevant to *this* question, which I may answer perfectly well by citing the cramped condition of my footwear, a sudden fancy to stretch my whole body, etc. Pressed by an interlocutor (e.g., from a psychology department) to say *how* it was that *I* brought it about that my toes wiggled, I could not intelligibly respond by citing antecedent physiological events in however long a causal chain right back to the neurons, because *that* kind of account does not mention me *as a person*, but only parts of my body. The latter sort of account can perfectly well take care of involuntary wigglings (or movements), but it cannot tell us how *I* could have wiggled my toes without knowing the least thing about my neurons, nor having any conscious control over their firing patterns. Whilst various parts of my body may be doing many different and wonderful things involved with my toes' wiggling, it is not *I* who am doing these things. All *I* am doing is wiggling my toes. That is as much a fact of our logical grammar as it is a fact about the world. We do not need to hypostatise a pseudo-entity called 'the will' to 'explain' how I wiggle my toes when I want to. It is not 'my will' that wiggles my toes for me. I wiggle them. And neither myself nor my will can succumb to description in terms of a computer's 'executive system', as various cognitivists would like to propose.[83]

Finally, on the topic of mental images. Ryle showed how mental picturings may be described not in terms of really seeing real pictures of whatever the mental picturings are showing. Rather, it must be construed in terms of *seeming to see* real pictures. After all, no *real* picture need be present for one to have a mental picture. So, one may now inquire: in *what* does the 'describing of a mental image' consist? I'm not really sure that I can give this a *thorough* response, but at least the following can be said: I am articulating a perceptual report over whose truth-value I am claiming sovereignty. But surely in order to 'report' something one must be engaged in something like acknowledging standards so as to distinguish between reporting and misreporting, reporting it correctly and making a mistake in one's report. In the case of one's mental images, there is no way to find out whether one has been reporting or misreporting, so how can we sustain the logical appropriateness of the ascription of 'reporting' to the case of describing one's mental image? Could we even now be happy with the concept of 'describing' in this connection? What holds for *reporting*, in this argument, holds also for *describing*.

One example of an undecidable consequence, attendant upon arguing that in telling you about my mental image I am describing something seen, would be the following. I tell you about my mental image, but you then ask me for more specific details about what it was I was picturing to myself. How are you to know whether my new description is a description of the missing details of the *old* image, or of a *new* one summoned to my aid? How could I be claimed *alone* to be in a position to say that the new one was identical to the old one? What standard of comparison could I use or appeal to in justification of any such claim? Wittgenstein declares:

> What is the criterion for the sameness of two images? What is the criterion for redness of an image? For me, when it is someone else's image: what he says and does. For myself, when it is my image: nothing. And what goes for 'red' also goes for 'same'.[84]

Here is a singular set of cases in which the truthfulness of the avowing agent guarantees the truth of his assertion. For other types of reports in the society (in *any* society), a speaker may be taken to have been speaking truthfully (sincerely) in offering them, but he could still be taken to be mistaken, wrong or simply deceived. For the present case of mental-image reporting/describing/telling, it is unintelligible to doubt the applicability of the report without *eo ipso* doubting the truthfulness of the speaker, the sincerity with which it is being offered. For where could a charge of 'having been mistaken' take hold here?

I do not believe that current cognitive theories about the 'etiology of behaviour', about 'discursive representations' embodied in, and for, the CNS, and about the eliminability of mental-image talk in favour of brain-talk, constitute adequate theories of mind. Indeed, I am not sure that what we require is a theory so much as an *explication* in this domain. However, any adequate explication is bound to constrain theory-constructions of the future, if such there be.

NOTES

1. John R. Anderson, *Language, Memory and Thought* (New York: LEA/John Wiley, 1976) pp. 15–16.
2. Jerry A. Fodor, *The Language of Thought* (New York: T. Crowell, 1975) p. 33. (Hence *L of T*).
3. Aaron V. Cicourel, *Cognitive Sociology* (Harmondsworth: Penguin, 1973).
4. Fodor, *L of T.*, pp. 73–4.
5. Ibid., p. 75.
6. Ibid., p. 123.
7. Ibid., p. 177.
8. Ibid., p. ix (Preface).
9. Ibid.
10. Ibid., p. 31.
11. Ibid., p. 28.
12. Ibid., p. 31.
13. Ibid.
14. Ibid., p. 32.
15. Ibid., p. 67.
16. For some elaboration on this essentially Rylean/Wittgensteinian point, see my *The Social Construction of Mind* (London: Macmillan, 1979) ch. 2.
17. Fodor, *L of T.*, p. 63.
18. Ibid., p. 179.
19. Hilary Putnam, 'Minds and Machines' in S. Hook, (ed.), *Dimensions of Mind* (London: Collier-Macmillan, 1960); 'Brains and Behavior' in

R.J. Butler (ed.), *Analytical Philosophy*, vol. 2 (Oxford: Blackwell, 1965), and 'The Mental Life of Some Machines' in H.-N. Castaneda (ed.), *Intentionality, Minds and Perception* (Detroit: Wayne State University Press, 1966). For an excellent Wittgensteinian counterpoint to these arguments, although not addressed to Putnam's work in particular, see J.F.M. Hunter, 'Wittgenstein and Materialism', *Mind*, vol. 86, no. 344, October 1977.

20. Putnam, 'Minds and Machines', p. 156.
21. Ibid., p. 157.
22. J.A. Fodor, *Psychological Explanation* (New York: Random House, 1968) p. 45. It is worth pausing to consider, in this connection, Fodor's following argument: 'This is to say, in effect, that whether actions whose definition requires reference to the motives, reasons, or intentions of the agent can be causally explained *depends upon whether physiologically sufficient conditions for having motives, reasons, and intentions can be specified.*' (Ibid., italics added). The set of states of affairs properly characterisable in terms of someone's having any of an indefinite set of particular motives, reasons and intentions must itself be indefinite, and must contain reference to circumstantial matters quite distinct from the physiological: e.g., the tone of voice which contextually gives away an intention to do something, the diary entries detailing the preparations to poison someone betraying someone's motive, etc. The prospect of success for a regimentation of the antecedent physiological conditions of a human nervous system in respect of any of these occasions of ascription and/or avowal of motives, reasons or intentions is slim indeed. And why should they have any explanatory force whatever, unless they are supposed to correlate with 'having a reason for an action' falsely construed as a *mental state*. I may be in any number of 'states' quite independently of fulfilling the ascription criteria-in-context for 'having a reason' to do something (e.g., when your action gives me a reason to get angry with you).
23. Bernard Harrison, *Meaning and Structure: An Essay in the Philosophy of Language* (New York: Harper & Row, 1972), p. 124.
24. P.F. Strawson, *Individuals: An Essay in Descriptive Metaphysics* (London: Methuen, 1959). Endorsement of this central thesis does not commit me to endorsing every step in Strawson's defence of it.
25. J.F.M. Hunter, 'On How We Talk' in his *Essays After Wittgenstein* (Toronto: University of Toronto Press, 1973), p. 168.
26. Ibid.
27. Ibid.
28. Fodor, *L of T.*, p. 108.
29. Ibid., pp. 109–10.
30. Ibid., p. 111.
31. Ibid. One wonders why this 'message' does not *itself* require 'decoding', to be usable.
32. Putnam, 'Minds and Machines', p. 149. (In these distinctions drawn by Putnam we can locate some of the foundations for what became the philosophical-psychological doctrine of 'psycho-functionalism').
33. For example, in his apparent belief that investigations of neural microstructures and microprocesses can yield data to support the claim

that such microstructures realize computational (or machine-table) routines or subroutines *identifiable with human mental* (i.e., for him, 'logical') *states*. (See, e.g., ibid., pp. 158–9).

34. Fodor often stresses his 'literalness'; he is, after all, propounding a series of statements contributing to a *scientific* theory in his self-description. His text features various stipulations about scientificity, many deriving from a mechanistic epistemology (in his favouring of deterministic theories of human action) and a stubbornly behaviouristic reading of Ryle and even Wittgenstein. (Perhaps the first of Fodor's fellow cognitivists to point out the inadequacies in this treatment of Ryle, although little is said of the later Wittgenstein, was D.C. Dennett in his (partly critical) review of Fodor's *The Language of Thought*. See Dennett, 'A Cure for the Common Code?' in his *Brainstorms* (Vermont: Bradford Books, 1978); 'Ryle does not attempt, as Skinner does, to explicate mentalistic predicates '[just] in terms of stimulus and response variables' (*L of T.*, p. 8). On the contrary, his explications are typically replete with intentionalist idioms.' (Dennett, p. 95).) On Fodor's 'literalness', see *L of T.*, p. 76.

35. Fodor, *L of T.*, p. 106. Note how this formulation is left as a general truism, presumably descriptive of an invariant *state* of a speaker who eventually says something. I would want to claim that the ascription-conditions for a predicate such as someone's 'having something to say' are quite occasioned, not invariantly present in cases in which someone starts to say something!

36. Fodor, *L of T.*, p. 103.

37. Fodor, *Psychological Explanation*, p. 3.

38. Ibid. Note that Fodor does not here distinguish between *physical* and *cultural* environments.

39. Ibid., p. 28.

40. Ibid., p. 29. Fodor, like Richard Gregory in his famous *Eye and Brain* (London: Weidenfeld & Nicholson, 1977 edn), esp. pp. 13–14, favours a neo-Helmholtzian view of perception in terms of 'unconscious inferences'. It is against this sort of view of perception that Ryle developed, in various places, his attack on the 'intellectualist legend'.

41. Ibid., p. 28. For a useful discussion of this issue, see Richard Rorty, 'Wittgensteinian Philosophy and Empirical Psychology', *Philosophical Studies*, vol. 31, no. 3, 1977. Rorty's critique of Fodor's neo-Helmholtzian version of recognising the 'same' in the 'different' is cogent, even though he proceeds in this article to endorse Dodwell's version of a computer-analogical psychofunctionalism. In his *Philosophy and the Mirror of Nature*, Rorty appears to endorse the general theoretical framework which Fodor introduces in his *Language of Thought* for cognitive studies, although it is a brief discussion in which contrary views are not themselves raised against these latest formulations by Fodor which, I think, constitute elaborations and developments of the basic themes of his earlier *Psychological Explanation*, especially its support for neo-Helmholtzian and Chomskian themes in perception and language-use studies.

42. In my view, the phenomena grouped under the heading of 'perceptual

constancy' do not form a coherent theoretical class amenable to coherent generalising explanation of an etiological kind. Defending this claim, however, would take me too far away from the main topic, which is to review and criticise existing cognitivist claims to have a coherent theory of such matters. It is perfectly possible that my own views are themselves false; but this in no sense affects my arguments against available views. It only leaves me wondering where 'theory' can go in this field.

43. Fodor, *L of T.*, pp. 73–4. I confess to finding the use of the concept of 'description' in this context utterly baffling.

44. Ibid., p. 74, n. 15 (Italics in original). Here, Fodor attempts to circumvent the objection that analytically specified rules are arrived at by independent methods of purposeful codification, bearing an utterly unknown resemblance to whatever rules a speaker might genuinely 'know' and thus could only be 'in accord' with what they say and do. (All of this derives from Fodor's uncritical acceptance of Chomsky's notion of 'unconscious mental representations of rules of grammar'. For an excellent critique of this and related views of Chomsky, see David E. Cooper, *Knowledge of Language* (New York: Humanities Press, 1975).

45. Ibid., p. 73.

46. Hunter, 'On How We Talk'.

47. Ibid., p. 167.

48. Ibid.

49. Norman Malcolm, 'Thinking' in E. Leinfeller *et al.,* (eds), *Wittgenstein and his Impact on Contemporary Thought, Proceedings of the Second International Wittgenstein Symposium* (Vienna: Holder-Pichler-Tempsky, 1978), pp. 415–16.

50. For a cognate, though slightly differing, version of the computational theory of action and cognition, see Zenon Pylyshyn's essays, 'Mind, Machines and Phenomenology', *Cognition*, vol. 3, no. 1, 1974–5 and 'Computation and Cognition: Issues in the Foundation of Cognitive Science', *The Behavioral and Brain Sciences*, vol. 3, no. 1, March 1980. (A Special Issue on Foundations of Cognitive Science, with two other major papers from Chomsky and Fodor respectively).

51. Michael Polanyi, *Personal Knowledge* (Phoenix: University of Chicago Press, 1958) ch. 4.

52. G.P. Baker and P.M.S. Hacker, *Wittgenstein: Understanding and Meaning*, vol. 1 (Oxford: Basil Blackwell/Chicago: University of Chicago Press, 1980) p. 276. (See the entire discussion of 'understanding new sentences', pp. 274–9).

53. See, *inter alia*, Margaret Boden's *Artificial Intelligence and Natural Man* (New York: Basic Books, 1977), and Joseph Weizenbaum's *Computer Power and Human Reason* (San Francisco: W.H. Freeman & Co., 1976).

54. On his SHRDLU program, see Terry Winograd, *Understanding Natural Language* (New York: Academic Press, 1972). On his ACT program, see J.R. Anderson, *Language, Memory and Thought* (New York: LEA/Wiley, 1976). On his ELIZA program, see Weizenbaum. On his STUDENT program, see D.G. Bobrow, 'Natural Language Input for a Computer Problem-Solving System' in M. Minsky (ed.), *Semantic Information*

Processing (Cambridge, Mass.: M.I.T. Press, 1968).
55. Weizenbaum, *Computer Power*, p. 136.
56. Daniel C. Dennett, *Brainstorms: Philosophical Essays on Mind and Psychology* (Vermont: Bradford Books, 1978), p. 107.
57. Ibid.
58. Ibid., p. 105.
59. Ibid., p. xix.
60. Ibid., p. xvii.
61. Ibid., p. xx. Dennett writes: 'the *attribute, being-in-pain*, is not a well-behaved theoretical attribute'. But whoever thought that it was?
62. Ibid.
63. On this, see P.S. Churchland, 'A Perspective on Mind-Brain Research', *Journal of Philosophy*, vol. 77, no. 4, April 1980.
64. C.E. Shannon and W. Weaver, *The Mathematical Theory of Communication* (Urbana: University of Illinois Press, 1949).
65. L. Brillouin, *Science and Information Theory* (New York: Academic Press, 1956). Cited in Churchland, 'Mind-Brain Research'.
66. Dennett, *Brainstorms*, p. 110.
67. Ibid., p. 114.
68. L. Weiskrantz (from *Proc. R. Soc. B.*, 171, 1968, p. 336) as cited in Ragnar Granit, *The Purposive Brain* (Cambridge, Mass: M.I.T. Press, 1977), p. 206.
69. Granit, *The Purposive Brain*, p. 199.
70. J.Y. Lettvin, H. Maturana, W.S. McCulloch and W.H. Pitts, 'What the Frog's Eye Tells the Frog's Brain', *Proceedings, IRE*, vol. 47, 1959.
71. Michael A. Arbib, *The Metaphorical Brain* (New York: John Wiley, 1972), p. 45.
72. Lettvin *et al* 'The Frog's Eye', p. 1950.
73. Dennett, *Brainstorms*, p. 114.
74. Ibid., p. 102.
75. J. Coulter, 'Theoretical Problems of Cognitive Science', *Inquiry*, (vol. 25, 1982). Dennett argues for the logicality of conceiving of mental images as information-bearing neural structures. He claims that when people have what to them are 'mental images', they are merely to be described as *believing* that they have such things. Calling peoples' avowals and subsequent other conduct following the having of a mental image '*B*-manifolds', Dennett argues that if these belief-manifolds 'turn out to be caused by things in the brain lacking the peculiar features of images, then the scientific iconophobe will turn out to be right, and we will have to say that that person's B-manifolds are composed of (largely) false beliefs, what one might call systematically illusory beliefs.' (Dennett, *Brainstorm*, p. 187). I have argued ('Theoretical Problems of Cognitive Science') that mental-image avowals are *not* belief-avowals in logical grammar, and that Dennett's eliminative materialist gambit of so reconceiving of them is *ab initio* ungrounded and arbitrary. Moreover, it subserves an incoherent account in which brain events/functions, which may well enable us to have mental images, are *identified* with such images. This is as mistaken as proposing that because it is our vocal

cords which enable us to produce utterances when we use them, therefore our vocal cords are *identical to* our utterances. On what grounds
could Dennett justify a conceptual move from characterising something
as a 'cause' of *X* to characterising that thing (thereby) as *identical* to *X*?

76. Dennett, *Brainstorms*, ch. 11.

77. Ibid., p. 225. Cf. Hunter's sensitive elucidation of the ordinary concept of
'pain' in his *Essays After Wittgenstein*, ch. 6.

78. John R. Searle, 'Minds, Brains and Programs', *The Behavioral and Brain
Sciences*, vol. 3, no. 3, September 1980, pp. 417–57 (including 27 brief
commentaries, and the author's response, 'Intrinsic Intentionality').
Searle's argument appears to me to rest upon the claim that experiential
talk about persons (by persons) is based upon an 'emergent' property of
their physico-chemical make-up, viz., their capacity for *having experiences*.
Their experiential life is not explicable even if we assume their conduct
and 'cognition' to instantiate a program, since a distinction may be
drawn between manipulating uninterpreted formal symbols according
to a set of directions converted into a set of electronic (or mechanical)
determinants (as in artificial-intelligence computer simulations of human
speech, and in machine-translation computers), on the one hand, and
attaching a semantic content to the symbols (e.g., being able to visualise
for oneself the referents of some of them, being able to use them in new
contexts and utterances quite spontaneously, etc.), on the other. Simulations of experiencers do not themselves experience. I should add that
I think some elements of Searle's argument are very convincing, but I
have reservations about his assertion that it makes perfect sense to say
'my brain understands English' (ibid., p. 451); for some arguments
about brains' 'recognising' and 'thinking' or 'having thoughts', see my
'The Brain as Agent', *Human Studies*, vol. 2, no. 4, October 1979).

79. Lynne Rudder Baker, 'Why Computers Can't Act', *American Philosophical
Quarterly*, vol. 18, no. 2, April 1981. She writes: 'Thus, a crucial difference
between machines and self-conscious beings is this: for self-conscious beings
there is an irreducible distinction between genuine self-consciousness and
consciousness of someone-who-is-in-fact-myself; for machines, on the other
hand, there is no corresponding distinction between say, genuine self-
scanning and scanning a unit-which-is-in-fact-itself – just as in the case of
self-defrosting refrigerators, there is no distinction between genuine self-
defrosting and defrosting a refrigerator-which-is-in-fact itself.' (p. 162). I
find the arguments in this paper utterly ingenious and compelling.

80. For some details, see Margaret Boden, *Artificial Intelligence and Natural Man*
(New York: Basic Books, 1977), pp. 434–44.

81. See my *The Social Construction of Mind* (London: Macmillan, 1979), ch. 2.

82. J.F.M. Hunter, ' "Forms of Life" in Wittgenstein's *Philosophical Investigations*' in E.D. Klemke (ed.), *Essays on Wittgenstein* (Urbana: University
of Illinois Press, 1971), p. 285.

83. For example, Ulrich Neisser, in his *Cognitive Psychology* (New York:
Appleton, 1967).

84. Ludwig Wittgenstein, *Philosophical Investigations*, trans. G.E.M. Anscombe
(Oxford: Basil Blackwell, 1968), para. 377.

2 On token physicalism and anomalous monism

The theory of token physicalism may be stated thus: for any given occasion on which you or I are actually in mental state M (say, in a state of *pain*), being in that particular mental state is *identical to* being in brain (or CNS) state S. There is quite a large philosophical literature dealing with this claim;[1] I refer to it here as a 'theory' in recognition of its research-guiding function in some recent neuroscientific work. For example, in his paper 'From Neuron to Behavior and Mentation', Mario Bunge asserts that 'thinking is identical with (reducible to without remainder) the activities (functions) of certain neural systems.'[2] Bunge clearly had in mind here something like the case in which one may engage in 'silent soliloquy' or 'interior monologue'. (We shall return to discuss interior monologue in detail in a later section of the present work dealing with 'thinking'.)

The token-token identity theory is contrasted to the *type-type* identity theory, according to which any given *type* of mental state (as distinct from a given instance of such a state) is identified with a *type* of brain state.[3] Such a view is congenial to the pursuit of formulating strict psychophysiological laws in which, e.g., *pain* is nomologically connected to *C-fibre firing*, and ultimately reducible to it. A major problem for type-type theory is articulated by Saul Kripke in a now classic discussion.[4] Kripke demonstrated that theoretical identities generated out of scientific research (e.g., the identity of heat with molecular motion, the identity of pure gold with any element with atomic number 79) are *a posteriori* necessities. That is, once accepted as facts, the identities are incorrigible even though discovered by empirical analysis and not solely by

43

a priori reflection. In *any* possible world, if an element is gold then it is necessarily also an element with atomic number 79; otherwise, we are not conceiving of the element we properly refer to as *gold*. The natural-kind type 'gold' and the natural-kind property of 'having atomic number 79' are not distinguishable once established as mutually constitutive. The case of a mental state such as pain, however, poses an intractable problem for such an argument. For, while heat and gold can be defined independently of the ways in which they may appear to people (heat by the presence of molecular motion, gold by the determination that the element has the atomic number 79), a mental state such as pain consists in the way in which it appears, in which it is felt. Unlike heat, which can be said to exist independently of creatures who can feel the *sensation of* heat (imagine a planet devoid of life but with objects whose molecules are appropriately agitated), in the case of *pain* there is no difference between the *sensation of* pain and pain itself. (We shall accept for the present argument the equation of 'sensations' with 'mental states'). Thus, concludes Kripke, if there were beings with C-fibres which were stimulated, then, according to the (properly stated type-type identity theory) such beings could not but be in pain *whether they were conscious of it or not*, which is a contradiction.[5]

The demonstrated *necessity* (albeit *a posteriori*) in the case of theoretical identities in science breaks down in the case of mental states and physical states, and, along with it, the type-type identity thesis for such states. In a possible world in which God created C-fibre stimulation, He must do something in addition to this for the stimulation to be felt as pain (rather than, say, as a tickle or as nothing at all): He must enable His creatures to experience the C-fibre stimulation in a specific way (i.e., *as pain*). Therefore, 'the relation between the pain God creates and the stimulation of C-fibres cannot be identity.'[6]

Donald Davidson's thesis of Anomalous Monism[7] is a classical statement of a *token-token* version of the physicalist doctrine. Davidson eschews the possibility of closure in lawful explanations of the relations between mental states and physical states:

We must conclude, I think, that nomological slack between the mental and the physical is essential as long as we conceive of man as a rational animal.[8]

Indeed, if we are to conceive of man as *a conscious, sentient being*, Kripke's argument against type-type identities and strict psychophysiological laws of a reductionist sort can take hold, as we have seen. Davidson's gambit is to propose that, although there cannot be tight psychophysiological laws due to the 'disparate commitments of the mental and physical schemes'[9] of description and explanation in a language with mental and physical predicates, nonetheless

> we see that it is possible to know that a mental event is identical with some physical event without knowing which one (in the sense of being able to give it a unique physical description that brings it under a relevant law) . . . . Mental events as a class cannot be explained by physical science; particular mental events can when we know particular identities.[10]

Presumably, on this account, one could expect to discover some particular neural process or state identical to some particular mental process or state without being committed to the claim that any or every occurrence of that same neural event is identical to any or every occurrence of that same mental event.

Does token-identity theory escape Kripke's objections against type-identity theory? Despite Colin McGinn's valiant attempt to show that it does, I beg to differ.[11]

I have no quarrel (in principle) with any of the following general claims (although empirical work could yet show them to be individually or severally false); (i) that pains are made possible by the functioning of nervous systems (using *pain* as the least question-begging case of a 'mental state or event'), (ii) that pains are functionally connected to other things (e.g., propensities to behave in certain ways such as rapidly shifting the organ from the pain-causing object, the presence of specific sorts of sensory inputs, the condition of nervous tissue, etc.) and (iii) that pains are not ethereal, incorporeal phenomena. However, nowhere in such a list of (defensible) propositions consonant with the token-token identity thesis is there any reference to the property of pains which perplexes us and which prompts the formulation of materialist doctrines in the first instance, viz., the property of the qualitative experience of pain.

To say that some particular pain (a token of the type 'pain') is realised by some particular functional-state configuration or simply by C-fibre firing(s) (as tokens of the types 'neural states'), disavowing generalisable formulations of invariant connections, is still to say nothing about *how* such a particular configuration or firing generates within us the particular experience we have. Stated as an *identity* thesis, token-physicalism, like type-physicalism, renders invisible this special property of mental states precisely as Kripke had argued. (Some commentators have labelled this the 'qualia' problem.[12])

The problem may be formulated in this way: how can we hope to give a clear account in principle of how a network of complex physical relationships such as a central nervous system might enter into states which, at the same time, *both are and have experiences*? The inclination here is to urge that it is *not* the nervous system which has an experience of any specific kind – it is we *as persons* (or whole organisms) who have experiences (mental states). Even though we may localise any given experience of pain by, let us say, remarking that one's pain is in one's leg, still it is not one's leg that feels the pain, it is oneself as a person who feels it. I can feel a pain *in* my leg, but I cannot (in logical grammar) say that my leg (or the nerves in my leg) feel(s) pain. In line with this argument, what sense can be given to the assertion that it is my brain or CNS which feels pain, has a pain or experiences pain? Clearly, it is intelligible (and probably true) that it is my CNS which in operating normally enables *me* to experience whatever I actually experience. And yet in such a formulation there lies the possibility of a dualistic misreading, according to which there is a something extra, over and above my entire sensory apparatus, in addition to my neurophysiological equipment, whose experiential life is being (only) facilitated by such apparatus and equipment.

At junctures such as this, one feels the pull of the argument about 'emergent properties' and 'self-perceiving systems'. One would like to claim that (mental) experiences or sensations (like pain) are in some unknown sense emergent properties of living organisms with nervous systems, but of course we still require some account of the possibility of any such 'emergent properties' and of the possibility of a physical system that not only scans its own states but generates *qualia* in the process.

Neither token- nor type-physicalist materialisms spare us from these impulses, these cravings for a solution to the problem which our conceptual system poses for us when we reflect upon ourselves as beings consisting of molecules, cells, neurons (etc.) in a putatively law-governed system, and as beings who have consciousness, experience, a mental life. Davidson's Anomalous Monism captures the logico-grammatical disjunctions between physical-state-and-process talk and mental-experiential talk in a restricted manner: he sees the futility of mapping laws for the former domain onto specifications of the latter domain, and yet cannot shed the univocality and homogenising propensity of monistic-materialist dogma.

However, we *cannot* know 'particular identities' any more than we can know type identities in this domain because the notion of 'identity' begs too many questions, carries with it too many incoherent conceptual commitments in its wake, to function as it does elsewhere in science and practical reason. Recognising this, but failing to free ourselves from the materialistic-reductionist impulse which has come to such splendid fruition in other fields of human inquiry, we are almost inexorably drawn towards a paradox: if my CNS is not the locus for the feeling of my C-fibres firing, then what could be? And now we open the door to the non-physical or the super-physical, to the ethereal or the spiritual. And *still* we crave for an explanation of how *these* 'entities' could do what 'mere' physiological systems apparently could not, viz. experience pains, have mental images and so forth. Here is one way in which reason can be constrained almost against itself: I have a pain in my side – my C-fibres are firing so that *I* feel the pain in my side – this 'I' must be an additional component interior to me capable of serving as the subject of predicates denied to my CNS. (My C-fibres do not feel *themselves* firing, nor does *my brain* feel my C-fibres firing: only *I* can feel what C-fibres firing produces). And yet, of course, the reification and interior projection of the meaning of 'I' in such expressions is not only a logico-grammatical mistake ('I' is not a referring expression, nor is it a *name* for an object or property interior to or exterior to myself): it is also a theoretical manoeuvre which posits an unknown phenomenon about which the same order of questions can be asked, namely, how could *it* do my experiencing *for me*?

I believe that Wittgenstein tried with only partial success to alleviate our metaphysical hankerings after 'theoretical models' in this area of our conceptualisation. The intractability of the sensation/brain-state problem (the form in which most contemporary discussions of the psychoneural identity issue are couched) arises in large measure from the apparent residua in the Wittgensteinian success story for a whole array of putatively 'private mental states and processes'. Although Wittgenstein and those who followed his lead managed to re-unite pains, mental images and occurrent thoughts with public conditions for rational ascription, avowal and ratification, and to show that these concepts are far more complex as predicates than a 'label-for-private-object' story would permit, they could not allay the temptation to seize upon them as embarrassments for holistic materialism or as dwellers in some inner-space, ontological slum ripe for 'eliminative analysis'. Must we, then, settle (perhaps reluctantly) for a kind of residual dualism?

In one form, dualism is as benign a characterisation of the existence of nervous-system states and occurrences of pains as would be a dualism for the existence of vocal cords and the occurrence of things said with their assistance. Doctrinalised dualism, however, is not benign. It carries in its wake a series of commitments just as mechanistic and untenable as its materialist-monist twin. In so far as doctrinal dualism urges upon us the view that a pain, say, is in every respect like a physical *object*, only it doesn't happen to be physical, we are in trouble. It is the move to attribute specific sorts of properties to pains (and other mental 'residua') which encourages many philosophers, psychologists and neurophysiologists to rush into the reductionist camp. If we grant that pains are objects, then we shall either have to concede that they are fundamentally (neuro-) physical in nature *or* particles of ethereal mind-stuff. Here, the Wittgensteinian insistence upon mounting a critique of the practice of assimilating pains to a material-object language-game comes to the fore. The 'grammar' breaks down.

Token physicalism, and its expression in the doctrine of anomalous monism, begins by acknowledging a major principle often attributed to William of Occam: do not multiply 'entities' beyond necessity. However, we should seriously question not only the 'entification' of pains and other putative mental states at issue, but also the violation of another, perhaps less well-known principle of the Occamists: do not supply as your *explanans* an hypothesis which generates more difficulties for the rational understanding than the original *explanandum*. And pains are here to stay; it takes an anaesthetic, and not a metaphysical doctrine, to do away with them.

NOTES

1. See, *inter alia*, David Randall Luce, 'Mind-Body Identity and Psycho-Physical Correlation', *Philosophical Studies*, vol. 17, 1966; Thomas Nagel, 'Physicalism', *The Philosophical Review*, vol. 74, 1965; Jaegwon Kim, 'On the Psycho-Physical Identity Theory', *American Philosophical Quarterly*, vol. 3, 1966; D. Wiggins, 'Identity, Designation, Essentialism, and Physicalism', *Philosophia*, vol. 5, 1975; L. F. Mucciolo, 'The Identity Thesis and Neuropsychology', *Nous*, vol. 8, 1974, and the collection entitled *The Mind/Brain Identity Theory*, edited by C.V. Borst (London: Macmillan, 1970).
2. Mario Bunge, 'From Neuron to Behavior and Mentation: An Exercise in Levelmanship' in H.M. Pinsker and W.D. Willis Jr (eds), *Information Processing and the Nervous System* (New York: Raven Press, 1980), p. 14. Bunge does proceed to note, however, that neural processes cannot be exclusively constitutive of 'thoughts': he adds that *their* content is 'partially dependent on what others around you and before you have thought', (ibid.) leaving the theoretical door open for 'social psychology, sociology, history, etc.' (ibid.)
3. The type-type identity theory has been by far the most common form of the

psychoneural materialist thesis. It entails token-token identity claims, but the converse does not hold.

4. Saul Kripke, 'Naming and Necessity' in Donald Davidson & Gilbert Harman (eds), *Semantics of Natural Language* (Boston: D. Reidel, 1972).

5. Ibid., pp. 340–41.

6. Ibid., p. 341. (Because this is, I think, the crux of Kripke's argument against *any* form of the psychoneural identity thesis, I have omitted any reference to his (risky) notion of 'rigid designation' in this connection, although it is obviously related to his view that scientifically defined indiscernibles comprise *necessary* ('essential') relata when confirmed.)

7. Donald Davidson, 'Mental Events' in Ned Block (ed.), *Readings in Philosophy of Psychology* (Cambridge, Mass.: Harvard University Press, 1980).

8. Ibid., p. 117. Davidson is here attending to the basically Wittgensteinian insight that ascriptions of mental predicates to persons vary in respect of our assessments of the overall coherence of their conduct in its circumstances and in the light of standards of rationality therein applicable.

9. Ibid., p. 116.

10. Ibid., p. 118.

11. Colin McGinn, 'Anomalous Monism and Kripke's Cartesian Intuitions' in Block, *Readings in Philosophy*. McGinn gives no good reason for construing Kripke's 'intuitions' as Cartesian. He (Kripke) nowhere *endorses* a metaphysical dualism. Indeed, he states clearly that he believes the mind-brain problem to be 'wide open and extremely confusing' 'Naming and Necessity' (p. 355, n77).

12. See Sydney Shoemaker, 'Functionalism and Qualia' in Block, *Readings in Philosophy*. Shoemaker is careful to note that the 'qualia' problem does not involve most mental concepts/predicates. Indeed, as J.F.M. Hunter pointed out in his 'Wittgenstein and Materialism', in *Mind*, vol. 86, no. 344, October 1977, p. 519, forms of thinking have a 'vanishing phenomenology' when subjected to careful analysis.

3 On rules and human conduct

In contradistinction to a prevailing assumption in various cognitive studies, I shall argue here that propositional knowledge of 'rules' (either 'consciously' known or 'unconsciously' known) is *not* entailed by concept-acquisition and concept-use. Having attempted to establish this point, I shall then try to specify some important properties of 'rules' as these *actually* enter into domains of human conduct. Some of these properties stand in contrast to those tacitly taken to characterise 'rules of conduct' in theoretical accounts of human behaviour. Since I believe that the entire issue of rules is immensely perplexing, and in some ways highly obscure, I am guided here by work in ethnomethodology and ordinary-language philosophy for whom the topic has been, for many years, a central concern. However, a failure adequately to connect these matters with broader theoretical concerns in the human sciences has resulted in a virtual chasm separating those with a major intellectual interest in the relationship of 'rules' to 'behaviour'. The present essay is a bit of bridge-building, linking up some lines of thinking from several disciplines and noting the points of divergence where these may be amenable to correction.

It was noted in the discussion of cognitivism that determinate rules governing the production and recognition of words, utterances and activities formed the central components of the putative 'cognitive apparatus' of human beings. Grammars of concepts, sentence-formation, perception, etc., were programmatically treated as theoretical representations, not of some corpus of data alone, but of actual 'internal' representations constituting 'internalised' guidance systems involved in the arrays

51

of human performances in concrete situations. An abiding theme in studies based upon such abstract claims has been that the orderliness and organisation of the vast bulk of acculturated ('intelligent') conduct is inconceivable without adverting to such a mental machinery of rules. Moreover, in some sociological versions of 'socialisation', it is the crucial role of a process of 'internalisation of the norms of a culture' which serves as the complement for the psycholinguist's 'internalisation of the rules of grammar' and the cognitive psychologist's 'unconscious induction of rules of behaviour'. We shall need to address the whole issue of what could be meant by 'internalisation' afresh.

1 THE CALCULUS-OF-RULES MODEL

To develop a clear sense of the contrary positions being taken with regard to the role of 'rules' in actual language-use it is instructive to consider the following clear statements of the opposing positions. G. J. Warnock is especially trenchant in the presentation of his views:

> It may be the case that it would be possible in principle to express the grammar of, say, English in the form of a corpus of rules; it may even be the case, though it seems a much more extraordinary claim, that the meanings of English words and phrases might be expressed in the form of rules for their 'use' (more extraordinary, since it is deeply unclear what such rules would look like, or how there could be any determinate limit to their number). But that it might be possible to formulate such rules does not entail, though it seems often to be taken to, that there already are such rules, and still less that those who speak and understand English are in fact following rules in doing so. It is admitted that in some cases, no-one yet knows what the supposed rules actually are, and it is certain that many who speak the language do not know.[1]

Taking the contrary view, Noam Chomsky responds to a

similar objection to the one raised by Warnock as follows:

> 'Transformationalists' have argued that speakers have
> developed specific systems of grammatical rules, and have
> sought to explain, on this basis, innumerable facts about the
> form and interpretation of utterances. They have thus pro-
> vided substantial evidence for (and often against) specific
> hypotheses about the rules that speakers have developed.[2]

However, when one consults the analyses presented by transformationalists, they appear as impressively elegant *codifications* or
formalisations of ways in which the syntactical forms of different
possible phrases and sentences may be related to each other,
including a canonical form for simplified word-or-morpheme
strings from which the initial phrases and sentences felt to be
related may be derived by deletions, substitutions and other
'transformational operations': these are the 'deep structures'.
Reading these analyses, one is struck by the ways in which they
represent an extension of formal-logical analytical methods for
dealing with the structures of propositions and their relations in
logic; yet it is quite recently that our logician-linguists have sought
to transpose their formal codifications of abstract relationships in
their canonical forms directly into their minds or brains of those
whose utterances form the basis for their (idealised) orders of
'data'. No logician sought to project the propositional or predicate
calculi directly into the minds or brains of good reasoners or
winners of logical arguments, and yet contemporary analysts seek
to locate their canonical codifications within ordinary speaker-
hearers in the name of 'the standards and methods of scientific
inquiry'.[3]

What has happened here? Consider the logician Waismann's
careful proposals about subsuming a person's conduct under a
rule.[4] He takes as an example a case where someone is observed
writing a series of figures on a blackboard – 1, 4, 9, 16, 25 – and
an observer who is watching and trying to formulate a rule which
expresses the one being followed by the writer. A series of
extensionally equivalent rules is advanced by the observer, from

among which the writer can select the one as (defeasibly) characterising his actual performance-rule. These could include: choosing the first number at random, adding three to it, and proceeding with squares; listing the series of squares of the first five cardinals; writing the substitution for x in the first five integers working according to the formula $y = x^2$, and so on. Of course, the possibility is open that the writer simply wrote down whatever numbers 'came into his head', or chose the first number at random, began to follow a rule but made a mistake in writing, or some other variant on this alternative theme. Transposing the relevance of this point – the existence of diverse but extensionally equivalent axiomatic systems – to the domain of language-use, David Cooper has argued that in the case of ordinary speaking and hearing it is the *absence* of criteria for identifying which of some extensionally equivalent canonical versions is known and applied (if any) which bars the projection of grammars to actual speaker-hearers.[5]

A quite natural riposte to this kind of counter-argument is that it consigns language-acquisition and language-use to the theoretical domain of (neo)-behaviourism. Yet neither Warnock nor Cooper entertain that option, and since Brewer's justly celebrated paper, 'There is No Convincing Evidence for Operant or Classical Conditioning in Adult Humans',[6] it is perhaps just as well. (Unfortunately, Brewer believes that cognitivist and psycholinguistic projections of the sort under scrutiny here qualify as the proper heirs to psychological theory in this domain.) Although I think that there are strong grounds for suspicion of mechanistic S-R conditioning theories of acculturation generally, it is important to take stock of the fact that 'knowledge of a rule' is logically tied to behavioural displays of various sorts, including, e.g., formulating some version of it, consulting it, adjusting one's conduct by reference to it, holding someone responsible for ignoring or violating it, and the like. The behaviourists were always perfectly right to insist upon observable forms of conduct as criterial for the ascription and ratifiable avowal of 'abstract knowledge', even though they have tended to describe such conduct in unnecessarily austere and impoverishing ways (as body movements, as 'responses', as 'organismic output' etc.) That ordinary language-users do not *advert to* or *use*, *consult* or *follow*, rules of the sort outlined by transformational-generative grammarians (e.g., Equi-NP deletion, Tough-Movement, Affix-Hopping, etc.) is evidence *against* their knowing them, even though their linguistic conduct may be found to be *in accord with them*.

The transformationalist programme, which aims to specify a finite set of determinate rules for all and only all of the infinitely many possible-grammatical sentences in a natural language, is fundamentally a part of formal logic, and does not belong to a programme for embarking upon the empirically controlled study of language-use. And yet there remains, at the heart of the trans-formationalist problematic, the issue of *novel* sentence-production and understanding. The creativity and (disciplined) freedom of language-users to express themselves in new (previously unused or unheard) sentences/utterances is a fact which Chomsky and his colleagues turned against the behaviourists in psychology who sought to explain linguistic conduct with the use of a theoretical scheme ill-fitted to this critical aspect of that phenomenon.[7] What *are* we to make of the apparent leap from mechanism and into freedom displayed so prominently in this most mundane accomplishment of human beings: their capacity to express (and understand) new as well as old ideas in new ways? We certainly do not learn to come up with sentences of any kind by looking them up in a finite lexicon of sentence-tokens (whether such a lexicon is external or 'internal' to us). Sentences and utterances are indeed constructed from words and phrases strung together in comprehensible ways, but there are no recipes available for *this* type of constructive process, apart from guides to suffice for correction or preferential formulation, guides formulable *post hoc* and even codifiable in some measure by formal linguistics independently of actual socialisation practices in families. Skinner, Quine and others in the behaviourist camp do not appear to find the novel-sentence phenomenon especially significant, whereas Chomsky, Fodor and their colleagues locate it at the centre of their thinking. They do so, however, only by insisting that it *must* be construed after the fashion of a recipe-based process. The 'creativity' involved in novel-sentence production and comprehension is said to be 'rule-governed'[8] – not in the (weaker) sense of being amenable to formal study in terms of a logic of organisational options (syntactic, conceptual, etc.) but in the (stronger) sense of being subject in flight, as it were, to control by internally represented rules.

The research-motivating problem, then, which led to a good deal of the psychologising in linguistics (removing it progressively from its social and pragmatic contexts) was the following: How do we assemble and understand sentences we have never heard nor used before? But the question is being asked in a very special way, a way which would render sarcastic at best an answer such as: we do it by talking and listening. For the manner in which we are being asked to inspect this question so-formulated is critical to our receptivity to the ensuing programme of inquiry. We are simply not allowed to claim that we say and understand new sentences in the same way in which we say and understand *old* ones, for that would cut short the peculiar interest we are meant to have. Indeed, as I reflect upon the question, upon its *meaning*, it becomes clear that it is itself wholly theory-laden from the outset. We are, I think, to take it that the question means: How do we unconsciously deploy our internalised rules so as to come up with novel combinations of words to utter or to comprehend? On any other reading, nothing like the theoretical machinery of trans-formationalist-inspired psycholinguistics would be necessary, for if we took the question to be asking how we come by new things to say, or what strikes us so that we say things in new ways, then it will instantly be clear that a wide variety of vernacular answers are available. I think then, that the formulation of the question and its preferred interpretation adopted by many transformationalists who make psychological claims for their work *actually begs the very conceptual scheme under consideration*, with no clear warrant other than the scheme itself. After all, as Hunter has noted,[9] we ordinarily ask *how* something is done in general terms when we do not know how to do it – whereas most of us can, and do, speak creatively, come up with new ways of saying old as well as new things. In fact, it is strange to be told that we do this, and next to be told that what we might have taken as a spontaneous under-taking on our part turns out not just to have logical connections with rules, but to be determined by rules. A normal contrast we make is between saying something on the basis of a rule which tells us how to say it, and saying something that is original, spontaneous and creative. In violating this (logical) contrast, we are driven to locating the 'rules' in an esoteric space, the unconscious warehouse of the 'mind'. In sum, we must not think that when someone

> utters a sentence and *means* or *understands* it he is operating a calculus according to definite rules. . . .
>
> What do I call 'the rule by which he proceeds'? – The hypothesis that satisfactorily describes his use of words, which we observe; or the rule which he looks up when he uses signs; or the one which he gives us in reply if we ask him what his rule is? – But what if observation does not enable us to see any clear rule, and the question brings none to light? – For he did indeed give me a definition when I asked him what he understood by 'N', but he was prepared to withdraw and alter it. – So how am I to determine the rule according to which he is playing? He does not know it himself. – Or, to ask a better question: What meaning is the expression 'the rule by which he proceeds' supposed to have left to it here?[10]

The 'interior' controlling system of guiding rules thought to be essential to our understanding of novel-utterance production now appears to be a theoretical postulate of greater mysteriousness than the phenomenon for which it stands as an 'explanation'. For, not only do we find ourselves unable to decide upon warrantable criteria for projecting a set of rules from any extensionally equivalent series to the subject, but in addition we are now tacitly assigning to our 'rules' properties of determinate causation adequate only to *laws*. In fact, some recent philosophers of psychology have proposed that we can derive a sound thought-model for rules construed as determining systems from a consideration of how computers operate. Ned Block writes:

> A digital computer is a device one knows to be rule-governed, for the rules are inserted by us as part of the program. In the digital computer, some operations are accomplished 'automatically' by hard-wired circuitry, and not via the application of any represented rules . . . . Sometimes a rule causally controls reasoning 'automatically', in the way the machine language command 'ADD 1' causes the representation in a register to change, by the operation of hard-wired circuitry, and not by any process involving reasoning.[11]

In this way, Block seeks an exit from the dilemma of a regress of rules for interpreting rules for interpreting rules, *ad infinitum*, by locating the relevant rules as wired-in, state-switching commands. However, no theorist writing rules putatively facilitating the production of novel (as well as non-novel) utterances has sought to specify them in terms amenable to Block's state-switching commands; no theorist of human conduct has access to design information about the CNS remotely like the design information we have about digital computers, and no theorist has ever succeeded in arguing that all (or even an interesting subset) of rules proposed to capture the assignment of sense in language-use can be formulated as *algorithms*. More importantly, however, it has not been established that human beings and their conduct instantiate a programme even remotely analagous to those available for digital computational devices. No-one 'inserts' rules into people as part of their 'program' in anything but the most strained metaphorical sense. But here we are venturing into the territory of learning and acculturation theory, to which we must pay more detailed attention.

2 'INTERNALISING' NORMS AND RULES

Even though I have been arguing against a certain picture of persons as rule-governed, sentient automata, I do not want to

be taken to be claiming that human conduct cannot be understood as intricately bound up, in many varying ways, with rules.
We shall see further on how diverse and subtle are some of the
relationships between abstract rules and aspects of human
conduct, and how overly homogenising and simplifying are those
approaches which seek to constrain all or most of conduct into a
version which renders it into types of output derived from
internalised rules.

Just as we needed to make a distinction earlier between 'knowing that' and 'knowing how' in respect of forms of behaviour, to
show that even 'complex' forms (such as coming up with
previously unheard sentences) are often those for which the
appropriate kind of knowledge to ascribe to the subject is non-
propositional 'knowing *how*' rather than knowing-that (a rule
applies, etc.), now we must complement this distinction with one
that is wholly cognate – the distinction between 'learning how to'
and 'learning that'. The programming metaphor for acculturation in humans is precisely a *metaphor* because much of the learning which it construes as programming-with-rules is, in fact, *non*-
propositional learning *how*. Of course, there is a great deal of
learning-that characteristic of early socialisation (given a rich
enough basis in language acquisition on the part of the learner),
and some of this propositional learning is indeed the learning of
discursive statements about conduct, categorical declaratives,
proverbs, principles and rules of various sorts. However, for those
accomplishments of the child for which the programming
metaphor has been so literally construed in modern cognitivism
and philosophy of psychology, there is very little actual rule-
learning going on at all. The misassimilation of *all* learning to
learning-that is, I think, the unnoticed grounds for the proposal to
insist that children are engaged in inducing propositional rules
(for language, perception, etc.) even when the ordinary criteria
for ascribing such activities are lacking; the gambit which circum-
vents the lack of such appropriate criteria is to assert that the rule-
induction (the programming) is going on out of awareness,
unconsciously, and automatically.

I want to call this theoretical move the *discursive idealisation device*,

and to note that it has a counterpart in discussions of acculturation outside of psychology. I shall no longer be adducing arguments to show its unsoundness when added to the stipulations
about the unconscious; my concern now is with versions of
acculturation in which discursive idealisation is employed to
handle learning achievements without any appeal to the unconscious. Given the breakdown of (operant and classical)
conditioning approaches to acculturation, and the recurrent
problems raised by cognitivist assumptions, any advances in this
area will have to come to terms with the problem of the proper
role of propositional-knowledge acquisition and use *vis-à-vis* non-
propositional knowledge acquisition and 'use' in human learning.

In sociology, there is a cross-paradigmatic continuity in the
fundamental conceptualisation of what is involved in acculturation. From Durkheim to Parsons (and the structural-functional-
ist tradition broadly considered) to Berger and Luckmann (and
some other 'social-constructionists') to Habermas (perhaps
unique among critical theorists in the attention he has paid to
socialisation theory), a basic claim has been that children are
involved in the 'internalisation' of the 'norms' of the society's
culture (including its differentiated 'sub-' or 'micro-' cultures).
For Parsons, the human 'personality' is in large measure the
product of an 'internalization of systems of social objects',[12]
where what is meant by 'social objects' are the roles and norms of
the social order. For Berger and Luckmann:

> in the internalization of norms there is a progression from,
> 'Mummy is angry with me *now*' to, 'Mummy is angry with me
> *whenever* I spill the soup'. As additional significant others
> (father, grandmother, older sister, and so on) support the
> mother's negative attitude towards soup-spilling, the generality
> of the norm is subjectively extended. The decisive step comes
> when the child recognizes that *everybody* is against soup-spilling
> and the norm is generalized to, '*One* does not spill soup' – 'one'
> being himself as part of a generality that includes, in principle,
> *all* of society in so far as it is significant to the child.[13]

Although this simple sequence of scenarios is not intended to stand as a theory of acculturation in the domain of, e.g., eating conduct, it makes an instructive contrast in the way in which it features the attribution of progressively refined and generalised rule-like understandings (in discursive form) to 'the child's *consciousness*'.[14] At some determinate point it is claimed that there is a conscious realisation of the extension of the norm, which is duly reformulated into a proscriptive-obligatory, substantive rule ('One does not spill soup'). There is no longitudinal, empirical evidence to buttress this elementary and generalised description of a process of rule-acquisition, but of course parents *are* instrumental in formulating rules (e.g. in warnings, threats, advice and instruction sequences) for their children's benefit.

Explicitly formulated normative precepts certainly comprise a component of a child's (and adult's) propositional learning. (Berger and Luckmann, in company with most sociologists who discuss socialisation in a non-Freudian context, do not consider non-propositional learning; perhaps this is to be consigned to psychology.) Nonetheless, it remains unclear from the array of accounts of 'internalisation' exactly what is meant by this term, and to what extent it is being claimed that refrainings from negatively sanctioned conduct or performances in accord with normative standards on the part of neophytes are actually *facilitated* by a mastery of some set of explicit precepts. Does 'internalisation' mean, simply, 'learning'? 'Or learning-and-subsequently-using'? If the latter, which is presumably being implied, then a significant issue is being omitted: how is the child to figure out where and when the 'internalised norm' actually applies? Are there norms for applying norms? Cicourel, for example, is quite explicit about embracing this latter option:

> The actor must be endowed with mechanisms or basic procedures that permit him to identify settings which would lead to 'appropriate' invocation of norms, where *the norms would be surface rules and not basic to how the actor makes inferences about taking or making roles.*[15]

Cicourel's appeal to 'mechanisms' is quite intentionally cognitivist; his subscription to a psycholinguistic/cognitive mode of construing 'the actor's' endowment is elaborated in discussions of the relevance of transformationalist and cognitive theorising to the analysis of acculturation.[16] The problem of where and when abstract norms (those propositionally learnt – the 'surface' rules) might be applied or 'invoked' (reflectively? subvocally?) is settled by reference to hypothetical, 'internal' procedures which perform the function of guiding the child in the identification of a norm's appropriate domain and its relation to any present setting. The origin in socialisation practices of the putatively 'basic' mechanisms permitting the child to make inferences, recognise settings and grasp the applicability or otherwise of any given norm is not clearly articulated in Cicourel's account, and here he faces the same kind of difficulty as the cognitivists themselves: to give account of how the *basic* 'rules' are actually available to the child if not by discursive instruction.

Sacks, in the context of a subtle analysis of some acculturation functions of dirty jokes going the rounds amongst children, makes some characteristically astute observations about rule-learning in socialisation:

> the domain of a rule's *possible* application is not the same as the scope of its *actual proper* application. Instead, rules are to be used more narrowly; i.e., not each occasion on which any given rule might apply is an occasion on which it should be applied . . . . That poses a variety of distinct problems for children, since some of the time, in following a rule, they turn out to be behaving incorrectly and are then corrected or sanctioned by adults, and come to learn that they aren't freed from adult supervision by virtue of the fact that they follow the rules they're told. And they can't get a handle on the size of the problem; i.e., they can't come up with a systematic, general solution. They can only 'learn by experience' when a rule will turn out to be incorrectly applied.[17]

Whereas Cicourel locates the 'systematic, general solution' in the postulated internal controlling 'mechanisms', Sacks notes that there is *no* such general solution (e.g., some high-order algorithm). The lack of any guarantee persists throughout life in dealings with rules, although experience with similar orders of contexts and situations of action does undoubtedly serve to cancel possible over-extensions or misapplications of many rules known by persons in their daily lives. Sacks goes on to propose that there is a special artfulness in the management of rule-learning and rule-use between adults and children. As he notices:

> As adults characteristically use a rule to correct a child's intendedly rule-governed activity, so the child learns to use a rule to counterpose a proposed violation. Children learn (and get a special kick out of being able) to answer complaints about possible rule violations by introducing another applicable rule, which they offer as the thing which yielded the activity being treated as a violation.[18]

Not only are children routinely capable of the artful placing of a rule-formulation in the doing of excuses, but they often can come up with a rule to defend their adult-ascribed violative conduct, which was one they have been taught on some prior occasion by the very adult who is now threatening sanctions.[19] Turning the tables in this way, children begin to develop an appreciation for the 'open-textured' character of taught norms. Learning propositionally about the substantive rules of a cultural and moral order is indeed a significant aspect of acculturation, but it should not be thought of as a mechanical process akin to programming a computer with a set of algorithms: learning is accomplished in certain ways and for certain purposes, and is subject to the artful management of arrays of pragmatic contingencies in everyday life. It is this which forms the empirically examinable foundation for our abstract thinking about the role of rules in the acquisition of cultural knowledge. When it is ignored, it is all too easy to oversimplify and mechanise the nature of this mundane but complex process, and to homogenise or even render invisible the artful practices of both parents *and* children in coming to grips with a social order and its transmission.

3 THE UNDER-DETERMINATION OF PERFORMANCE BY RULES

Kant, among others, confronted a limitation upon the attempt to prescribe reason by rule. For Kant, the human ability to apply rules 'is a skill so deeply hidden in the human soul that we shall hardly guess the secret trick that nature here employs.'[20] Wittgenstein repeatedly emphasised the dependence of any rule upon a background of judgments and forms of training:

> Not only rules, but also examples are needed for establishing a practice. Our rules leave loop-holes open, and the practice has to speak for itself.
>
> We do not learn the practice of making empirical judgments by learning rules: we are taught *judgments* and their connexion with other judgments. A *totality* of judgments is made plausible to us.[21]

And Garfinkel, in his celebrated analysis of the *et cetera* property of rules of conduct, drew attention to the fact that aspects of the presupposed background judgments and expectancies are amenable to manipulation:

> That the work of bringing present circumstances under the rule of previously agreed activity is something contested should not be permitted to mask its pervasive and routine use as an ongoing and essential feature of 'actions in accord with common understandings'. This process, which I shall call a method for discovering agreement by eliciting or imposing a respect for the rule of practical circumstances, is a version of practical ethics. Although it has received little, if any, attention by social scientists, it is a matter of the most abiding and commonplace concern in everyday affairs and common sense theories of these. Adeptness in the deliberate manipulation of

et cetera considerations for the furtherance of specific advantages is an occupational talent of lawyers . . . however, . . . the method is general to the phenomenon of the society as a system of rule governed activities.[22]

The retrospective-prospective elaboration of the sense of any rule, of its intended domain, of its applicability and constituency, is a property of the actual use, invocation and appeal to rules in everyday affairs whose pervasiveness is now quite well documented – once Garfinkel pointed out its implications for extant theories of social order as rule-governed. Indeed, there are several studies whose chief objective is to specify the ways in which activities and the rules under which they could be situationally subsumed are *actually* related to each other.[23]

Even the most highly codified of human practices, such as games-with-rules, logical inference-making and mathematical reasoning, are, as Wittgenstein argued extensively, 'not everywhere circumscribed by rules'.[24] Background training, judgments and presuppositions enter into the circumstantial relevance of all rules for human practices. There is no rule in tennis which states how hard or high one is to hit the ball; there is no rule or set of rules which tell us what to do while figuring out which card(s) to play in poker, and so on. Those rules which *do* appear to be necessary to the conduct of some practice do not in themselves, in their formulation, dictate or specify *how* they are to be followed. And, as Lewis Carroll long ago pointed out in his famous paper, 'What the Tortoise Said to Achilles',[25] the act of drawing an inference cannot itself be represented in a logical rule; it is something that people must learn to *do*.[26] The logical and mathematical *must* is not a *must* of determinate and invariant prediction, but a decisive expression of our normative commitments in respect of logical and mathematical *activities* of certain sorts. As Wittgenstein put it, making a point similar to Carroll's:

You admit *this* – then you must admit *this* too. – He *must* admit it – and all the time it is possible that he does not admit it![27]

That people do, on the whole, acquire the capacities to undertake mathematical and logical tasks does not show that logic and
mathematics are somehow transcendentally guaranteed; they
work only in so far as *we* agree in our judgments and entertain the
'normal' sorts of background assumptions relevant to them.
Searle, in a succinct treatment of the indexicality of sense, has this
to say:

> Perhaps one might show, for example, that an arithmetical
> sentence such as '3 + 4 = 7' is not dependent on any contextual
> assumptions for the applicability of its literal meaning. Even
> here, however, it appears that certain assumptions about the
> nature of mathematical operations such as addition must be
> made in order to apply the literal meaning of the sentence.
> (Thus, in Wittgenstein's example, A = 3, B = 4, but
> A + B = 5)[28]

Wittgenstein's demonstration, to which Searle alludes, involves
seeing A and B in the following manner, and performing the
computation accordingly:[29]

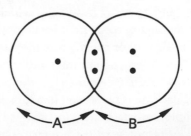

In his *Remarks on the Foundations of Mathematics*, Wittgenstein
presented various examples designed to break the hold on us of
the view that rule-following in mathematics is a matter of our
being inexorably determined in our way of approaching a topic
solely by the rule, as if the rule and it alone guided us to the

correct solution, which is somehow contained in the formulation of that rule. He shows how the proper use of rules depends upon a form of tacit or implicit acknowledgement of matters not themselves covered in any rule we may use or appeal to in doing our calculations or other forms of mathematical thinking. For example, he notes that the idea of locating a one-to-one correlation between some set of lines and some set of angles depends upon a method of projection which does not allow for any one of the lines to be treated as a fusion of two or more lines into one linking line:[30]

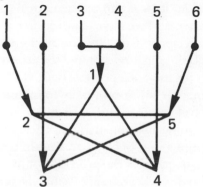

This is not the place to enter into a detailed exposition of Wittgenstein's views on mathematical proof and mathematical necessity. The examples selected from his writings on these matters are designed to help us to grasp to how deep an extent is our rule-ordered reasoning itself dependent upon assumptions and judgments which fall outside the rules we learn to apply. And, of course, they show as well how our sense of being *determined* by a rule rests upon a specific kind of taken-for-granted 'normalcy context' which is itself no more immutable than any other conventional practice we share. It is important to note, however, that the conventionality of mathematical and logical reason, whilst indeed contingent upon majority agreement and the adoption of a particularly stringent attitude toward error, is not of a piece with those more transparently conventional human practices. In both logic and mathematics, viewed as collections of practices, 'majority is right' cannot be laid down as a *principle of*

operation even though it is, of course, presupposed in the very functioning of those practices and the enforcement of operative standards. For Wittgenstein, the non-viability of any alternative to our systems of logic and mathematics is not a function of their having some transcendentally objective support, but a function of their rootedness in our matrices of practical action and practical reason, in the myriad of ways we have of counting, measuring, arguing, calculating and training novices, as well as in the natural facts of our environment, such as its relative constancies and variabilities. When we assess deviant systems of *non*-ratification of what we consider logical and mathematical necessities, we do so by *our* standards, and we have to appreciate that judgments of deviance can be reciprocated. What counts for us is that our rules of logic and mathematical reason and the practices they inform have *consequences* for us which pervade our lives, not that they rest upon extra-human or supramundane 'foundations'.[31]

In an earlier treatment of logicality and contextualisation,[32] I discussed (in a rather mentalistic way, I fear) the sort of background assumptions that become an invisible feature from the standpoint of participants in the practical routines of locating and ascribing irrationality.[33] In making visible the tacit supports, the implicit contextualisations which furnish arguments, proofs and utterances with their logicality or lack of it, ethnomethodologists are not so much challenging logical and mathematical formalisms as seeking to reveal what actually enables them to *work* for us. Yet, inasmuch as many contemporary theoreticians in the behavioural sciences have latched onto the notion of 'rule' in their analyses of and explanations of human behaviour, it is as well to recall that constitutive as well as preferential rules require supplementation by judgment and presupposition; it is in *this* sense that no calculus or grammar of rules, however extensive and explicit, can fully encompass the intelligibility of so much human conduct. That this is so even in those domains in which the notion of a *strict categoricity rule* applies only shows the radical character of the claim that such conduct is underdetermined by rules. None of which (need one say?) undermines in the least the usefulness of the concept of 'rule' in analysing conduct; it simply establishes a limit to the depth of any such analysis and reasserts once again the integrity of the human agent *vis-à-vis* totalising theoretical systems.

NOTES

1. G.J. Warnock, *The Object of Morality* (London: Methuen, 1971) pp. 48–9.
2. Noam Chomsky, *Reflections on Language* (New York: Pantheon Books, 1975) p. 251, n. 38.
3. Ibid.
4. Friedrich Waismann, *The Principles of Linguistic Philosophy*, ed. Rom Harré (London: Macmillan, 1965) p. 120 *et seq.*
5. David E. Cooper, *Knowledge of Language* (New York: Humanities Press, 1975), p. 57. I have found Cooper's book, especially his chapters on 'Rules and Rule-Following' and 'Dispositions and Knowledge', to be an excellent resource in tracking down these knotty problems.
6. William F. Brewer, 'There is No Convincing Evidence for Operant or Classical Conditioning in Adult Humans' in Walter B. Weimer and David S. Palermo (eds), *Cognition and the Symbolic Processes* (New York: LEA/Halsted, 1974). This must surely be one of the best-documented discussions and critiques of behaviouristic thinking in psychology ever written. Its concluding remark, that S-R psychology's foundation 'was one of sand' (p. 32), may yet generate some rebuttals, but I confess to a sense of relief that someone had undertaken such a thoroughgoing, empirically-documented critique of the field. Behavioural psychologists have been able to disregard many epistemological issues for too long; philosophers appear to have been reluctant to dig into the experimental literature in detail. We have Brewer to thank for raising these issues in connection with so large an experimental-literature review as to be imposing upon his critics.
7. Noam Chomsky, 'Review of B.F. Skinner's *Verbal Behavior*', *Language*, vol. 35, no. 1, 1959. Chomsky had earlier sharply distinguished his own views about linguistic theory from the position of L. Bloomfield, the leading American linguist who embraced behaviourism. L. Bloomfield, *Language* (New York: Holt, Rinehart & Winston, 1933).
8. Criticising the legacy of de Saussure, Chomsky writes, 'There is not a place in his scheme for rule-governed creativity of the kind involved in the ordinary everyday use of language. N. Chomsky, *Current Issues in Linguistic Theory* (The Hague: Mouton, 1964) p. 23.
9. J.F.M. Hunter, 'On How We Talk' in his *Essays After Wittgenstein* (Toronto: University of Toronto Press, 1973), Section 1.
10. Ludwig Wittgenstein, *Philosophical Investigations*, trans. G.E.M. Anscombe (Oxford: Basil Blackwell, 1968) paras 81 and 82. One quibble might be with Wittgenstein's query: 'So how am I to determine the rule *according to which* he is playing? He does not know it himself.' [My italics].

I think that it is possible to specify rules with which persons' conduct is in non-trivial accord independently of their state of knowledge, even though (and here, I believe, is Wittgenstein's real point) one cannot claim to have discovered the rule which he was *following* or by which his conduct was actually *guided*.

11. Ned Block, 'What is Philosophy of Psychology?' in N. Block (ed.), *Readings in Philosophy of Psychology* (Cambridge, Mass.: Harvard University Press, 1980): vol. 1 p. 5. Cf. Jerry Fodor, *The Language of Thought* (New York: T. Crowell, 1975) pp. 65–79. Hunter, by contrast, has serious reservations about the *literal* applicability of the concept of 'rule-following' to mechanical devices, including computers. He notes: 'Such a device operates in a regular way; but why should we say it follows a rule? It neither remembers nor forgets the rule, neither understands nor misunderstands its application, neither applies it carefully nor carelessly.' (Hunter, 'On How We Talk', p. 166). Would the machine-language command mentioned by Block count as a rule which the machine *follows?* I find the notion of 'following' here somewhat stretched, even metaphorical, and certainly too equivocal to establish Block's point about the conceivability of algorithmic generation of conduct by a nervous-system construed as computational.

12. Talcott Parsons and Robert F. Bales, *Family Socialisation and Interaction Process* (New York: Free Press, 1955) p. 54.

13. Peter L. Berger and Thomas Luckmann, *The Social Construction of Reality* (London: Allen Lane, Penguin Press, 1967) pp. 152–3. The closeness of Berger and Luckmann's treatment to that of G.H. Mead is clear (and acknowledged).

14. Ibid., p. 152 [Italics added].

15. Aaron V. Cicourel, 'Interpretive Procedures and Normative Rules in the Negotiation of Status and Role' in his *Cognitive Sociology* (New York: Free Press, 1974) p. 27.

16. Ibid. See especially ch. 2: 'The Acquisition of Social Structure: Towards a Developmental Sociology of Language and Meaning' and ch. 3: 'Generative Semantics and the Structure of Social Interaction'.

17. Harvey Sacks, 'Some Technical Considerations of a Dirty Joke' in Jim Schenkein (ed.), *Studies in the Organisation of Conversational Interaction* (New York: Academic Press, 1978) pp. 264–65.

18. Ibid., p. 265.

19. Ibid.

20. Kant, *Critique of Pure Reason*, trans. N.K. Smith (London: Macmillan, 1964) A141.

21. Ludwig Wittgenstein, *On Certainty*, G.E.M. Anscombe and G.H. von Wright (eds), trans. D. Paul and G.E.M. Anscombe (Oxford: Basil Blackwell, 1974) paras 139, 140.

22. Harold Garfinkel, *Studies in Ethnomethodology* (New Jersey: Prentice-Hall, 1967) p. 74.

23. See, *inter alia*, Garfinkel on 'Following Coding Instructions' (in *Ethnomethodology*, pp. 18–24); D.L. Wieder, *Language and Social Reality: The Case of Telling the Convict Code* (The Hague: Mouton, 1975);

D.L. Wieder, 'On Meaning By Rule' in Jack D. Douglas (ed.), *Understanding Everyday Life* (Chicago: Aldine, 1970); Don H. Zimmerman, 'The Practicalities of Rule Use' (ibid.); Don H. Zimmerman and Melvin Pollner, 'The Everyday World as a Phenomenon' (ibid.), and the excellent debate between Phillips and Heritage in *Sociology*, vol. 12, no. 1, January 1978 (Special Issue: Language and Practical Reasoning).

24. Wittgenstein, *Phil. Inv.*, para. 68.

25. Lewis Carroll, 'What the Tortoise said to Achilles', *Complete Works*, (Nonesuch Press, nd.). Carroll describes the encounter between the Tortoise and Achilles to consist of an interchange in which Achilles attempts to secure the Tortoise's agreement on grounds of logical compulsion to an inference (Z) from propositions (A) and (B). The Tortoise insists upon interpolating additional hypothetical propositions of the form: 'If (A) and (B) and . . . are true, then (Z) between the propositions (A) and (B) and the inferential conclusion (Z), such that every time agreement is reached on one of the interpolated propositions (e.g., proposition (C): If (A) and (B) are true, then (Z)) it is to be recorded as yet another proposition (i.e., proposition (D): If (A) and (B) and (C) are true, then (Z)), *ad infinitum*. Until the Tortoise grants the infinitely extendable set of interpolated propositions, he claims, then he has not been compelled to accept (Z).

26. See Winch's discussion in his *The Idea of a Social Science and Its Relation to Philosophy* (London: Routledge & Kegan Paul, 1958) pp. 55–7. Cf. L. Wittgenstein, *Remarks on the Foundations of Mathematics*, eds G.II. von Wright, R. Rhees and G.E.M. Anscombe: trans. G.E.M. Anscombe (Cambridge, Mass.: M.I.T. Press, 1972) paras 6–11.

27. Wittgenstein *Remarks*, para 51.

28. John R. Searle, 'Literal Meaning' in his *Expression and Meaning* (Cambridge: Cambridge University Press, 1979), pp. 131–2. [Edited to include footnote].

29. Ibid., p. 132. It should be noted that Wittgenstein's actual example is the following: he says that we have only to look at the figure below to see that $2 + 2 = 4$. But then if we look at the *adjacent* figure, we can see that $2 + 2 + 2 = 4$! (*Remarks*, para. 38).

30. Wittgenstein, *Remarks*, para. 40 (Angles and lines are numbered in my representation for the sake of greater clarity).
31. For some useful discussion, see David Pears, *Wittgenstein* (London: Fontana Modern Masters, 1971) pp. 135–40.
32. See my discussion of 'strategic contextualisation' in ch. 5 of *The Social Construction of Mind* (London: Macmillan, 1979).
33. For a much fuller treatment, with many novel insights, see David Helm, 'Conferring Membership: Interacting with "Incompetents" ', unpublished Ph.D. dissertation, Sociology Department, Boston University, 1981, chapter on 'Strategic Contextualisation'.

4 On 'traces', 'engrams' and memory models

Human beings are linked to their past, to their own autobiographies as living arrays and weavings of events, occasions, persons, things, by virtue of their capacities for memory. Our access to history is in some part made possible by our recollecting events and states of affairs and accounts of events and states of affairs. Memory functions are, and will be, topics for scientific study as well as topics for philosophical and practical analysis.

In the ensuing discussion, I am far from exhausting a vast and rich field of study. Indeed, I am not attempting to review much more than than a handful of (current and cogent) works on remembering in the sciences. My intention is limited: to raise some recalcitrant questions and some new ones for this domain of study, and to formulate an argument for the relevance of conceptual analysis to theory-construction and hypothesis-formation within it.

I am primarily interested in problems of conceptualisation which have arisen when theoreticians and researchers seek to construct 'models' and 'scientific explanations' for remembering (in humans, but also in animals). In particular, I want to try to arrive at an understanding of 'trace' theory (and metatheory), and some of its cognates, such as 'neural representation' theorising, 'storage' modelling and conceptions of 'engrams'. In doing this, I hope to become clearer about the epistemological issues involved and the structure of our overall paradigmatic 'picture' in this field. Endogenous and logical, more than exogenous and empirical, problems will preoccupy us in this exploration, but it is clear that the two are intertwined.

Memory is one of the natural capacities of human beings for which a particular explanatory model has long been thought appropriate: we have some experience and a 'trace' of it is generated and stored in our brains so that at some later date its 'activation' enables us to remember the original experience. Forgetting is thereby attributable to trace obliteration or degradation.

'Trace' or 'neural representation' theories of human memory have recently been subjected to a variety of criticisms, of which the following strike me as especially pertinent:

i. 'Occurrent' remembering (as contrasted with, *inter alia*, remembering in the sense of having learned and not forgotten something) is generally taken as a *unitary* sort of phenomenon. Munsat[1] and Malcolm[2] have both shown that even such a putatively paradigm case of occurrent remembering as 'suddenly remembering' cannot be given any *unitary* characterisation (without much arbitrary idealisation). Remembering is both polymorphous in its manifestations and contextually variable in its recognisability. Some action, utterance, gesture, mental image, etc., or any combination of these, cannot be claimed as a contextually invariant element *defining* or *fixing* the phenomenon of occurrent remembering. Moreover, remembering is a *defeasible* achievement, involving necessary reference to claims about personal implication or witnessing in the *past* which stand in need of actual or potential public ratification; there can be no *intrinsically* criterial memory events at all.[3]

ii. 'If the memory trace is thought of as a stored representation which facilitates reports of the past by becoming available, [sic] or causing some other representation to be available for inspection at the relevant time, then the process appears to be one of prompting rather than remembering. We have not explained remembering, but only a type of prompting which might then lead the person to remember.'[4] Moreover, the trace itself cannot carry with it its own identity as a *memory*-trace, as distinct, say, from an imagining or daydream, etc. To recognise the trace or its related representation *as a memory* would require something more than the trace itself.

iii. Trace theories are silent about *retrieval* mechanisms; since 'no one maintains that we do anything resembling rummaging through filing drawers when we are trying to remember something',[5] and since not all remembering is an outcome of *trying* to remember, the retrieval problem is recalcitrant.

iv. There are many cases of occurrent remembering for which the nature of an 'input' into any hypothesised neurological storage system is impossible to delineate empirically. 'We remember not only what we have seen, heard and been told, but what we thought, believed, intended, hoped; and also we sometimes do not remember the words we have heard or read, but do remember their sense [and] in doing so we are not working from one set of words which "comes back to us" '.[6] If all occurrent remembering required reading off the content from the (mental actualisation of the) trace of the input, then we should always have a clear picture or series of pictures unambiguously available as former intentions, beliefs, hopes and the like. This is clearly contrary to the ways in which we actually come to avow such matters.

v. Even in those particular instances in which someone claims to be producing an account of the past (based upon personal experience of what is recounted) by employing a method of describing what is unfolding 'in their mind's eye' – the paradigm case for representational theorising – there still remains the possibility, as Hunter has noted, that the person is not so much describing trace-generated images as he is 'illustrating the description . . . with mental pictures'[7] whilst giving it. The speculative explanation of (occurrent) *remembering* and the phenomena we (variously) identify in everyday life as such do not connect up. At best, trace theories depict a mechanised version of (variable) features of remembering; they neither fully describe nor explain the phenomenon under investigation.

If these objections are generally sound, and I think that they are, then trace or neural-representation theories of memory may be involved in *petitio principii* problems of a chronic kind, as well as being underdeveloped empirically. This is *not* to say that there are no serious experiments undertaken on memory. However, the adequacy of these researches seems itself dependent upon simply assuming without question the underlying validity of trace-storage models. Consider the following extract from a discussion of some pertinent work in this area:

> Begg and Paivio argue that *S*s recode concrete sentences into images and thus make errors in recognizing synonym substitutions; abstract sentences are not recoded into images and are supposed to be remembered in terms of the words themselves. Brewer argued, therefore, that abstract sentences can be used to make a crucial comparison between the memory for ideas approach and the memory for images approach. If abstract sentences are remembered in terms of underlying ideas, then *S*s in recall should make synonym substitution errors on these sentences, just as they do on concrete sentences. However, if abstract sentences are remembered as sequences of words, they should not show synonym substitutions. Brewer found that abstract sentences each written to contain a potential synonym show large numbers of synonym shifts in recall, just as concrete sentences do. *This finding supports the memory for ideas position that abstract sentences are transformed into ideas for storage.*[8]

This conclusion is hardly compelling, and the reasoning involved is suspect. Whilst there is no doubt that we may conjure up mental images when learning some (series of) sentence(s), whether concrete or abstract (which parameters themselves are quite vague as discriminators), it is a leap of inference to allege that we somehow *store* 'images' *in* our brains from which we (unconsciously) 'read off' the original sentences. There is nothing in this story which rationally relates to 'recognizing synonym substitutions', which is a specific undertaking/achievement in its own right. Moreover, there will be many occasions on which I may recall, due to some original purpose I had, a set of either concrete or abstract sentences in their original form (or in approximately their original form, depending upon my accuracy). For some other purpose, a rough paraphrase, the 'gist' or the 'idea' expressed in the originals may suffice. But what could it mean to assert that in remembering abstract sentences of any kind I am engaged in (or, rather, my brain is engaged in) 'storing' the 'ideas' they express? If all this means is that I can sometimes come up with different forms of words which more or less express the original ideas conveyed by the sample sentences, then it is uncontroversial – even trivial. However, a far more contentious theoretical claim is being advanced here; *viz.*, that my 'cerebral storage system' houses 'ideas' (expressed in what?) which serve as the traces of the original sentences, and it is these ideational traces which enable me to remember, albeit often inaccurately in so far as I do not detect various substitutions noted by an experimenter. For *this* particular claim, if it is coherent at all, no empirical evidence whatsoever has been presented. It is a purely stipulative conjecture. Brewer's 'finding' that some arbitrary set of abstract sentences 'show large numbers of synonym shifts in recall' is compatible with a host of interpretations, and in no way supports his conception of ideational transformation and storage in brains. My failure in a task of learning a series of sentences so that I could repeat them in their exact original form may be attributable to a variety of factors, including interest, familiarity with some terms and not others, degree of relatedness of sentence parts in my understanding, etc. Why should we accept that 'if abstract sentences are remembered as sequences of words, they should not show synonym substitutions'? I may try to recall the original sequence and fail to get it fully correct, or I may try to recall the sequence by thinking of what it expressed and work from there, or I may simply have misread the original sequence although not so wildly as to be utterly wrong about what it said. Nothing here bears on the claim about storage; in fact, it is impossible to conceive of a form of empirical research which could be brought to bear on a claim about brains storing 'ideas'. How and where could one look for these 'ideas' in the brain? My brain certainly functions normally so that I can, for the most part, remember what I have read, the ideas expressed in what I have read, and so on, but this does not show that my brain (somehow) transforms what I read into 'ideas' and stores these ideas away for future presentation to me. This is merely a fancy metaphorical way of redescribing a commonplace: I can remember often not only the particular form of words used but what the words *meant*, and I can sometimes come up with a version of an original form of words which preserves the initial sense but not the totality of the words used.

It is worth taking stock of the (logico-grammatical) fact that where I can *remember how* to do something (e.g., something I have learned to do) without this entailing that I can formulate this skill in *words*, the impulse to postulate stored traces or internal representation does not arise. I can remember how to swim, but nothing thereby prompts me to postulate some item of (learnt) propositional information, although I could if you like tell you some of the things that I do when I swim. The latter, of course, are not being remembered (necessarily). It does not make sense to say of me that I have literally *stored an ability to swim* somewhere inside me. Learning *how* and remembering *how* are achievements not in the least to be proven only by coming up with information in propositional form. Only on those occasions in which I can warrantably say that I 'remember how the song (poem, sonnet) *went*' do I need to buttress the (defeasible) claim by reciting from memory, by saying something that counts as a correct recitation of the song (poem, sonnet). However, let us consider remembering *that* (e.g., '*X* is the case, was the case') as our basic case in terms of which to assess trace-storage thinking.

Let us suppose that I (can) remember *that* such-and-such occurred at time t_1. Call this recollected thing an 'event' or 'occasion'. If we are to claim that my occurrent recollection at t_2 is facilitated by a stored impression, trace or representation of that 'event' or 'occasion', we have an obligation to specify some criteria by which (at least *in principle*) the trace or representation is describable. What, then, could we count as the 'elements' or 'components' or 'parts' of the 'whole' that was stored in some encoded form inside ourselves? How are we to demarcate the beginning, middle and end of one trace and the beginning, middle and end of some *other* trace? When we describe some event or occasion, even when we want to say that what we are doing is actually 'reading off' or 'describing the details of' a memory-image (a mental actualisation of the neural trace itself?), how are we to tell whether there is one, several or many traces facilitating this process? If memory-images and stored traces are in *one-to-one correspondence* (which is simply an assumption without criteria), then the trace makes itself felt only on those occasions when a mental image is involved in our occurrent remembering. Other forms of remembering (e.g., when I simply *say* what took place, am right about it, and no images at all were avowable in connection with this) have no need of trace-theoretic support, if such a version is correct. But let us consider the individuation of a 'stored representation' somewhat more fully.

Suppose that I am describing to you what (I claim) took place in one of my classes several years ago. There are witnesses still around and independent records to corroborate my account, to enable you to have confidence in its being a *memory* and not, say, an imagining, dream-report or fabrication. Now, suppose that you accompany me as I meet several friends and report the same recollection to them in slightly different words each time, but each time claim to be describing the *same* recollection (perhaps I might claim to be describing the same memory-images each time, perhaps not). How could one proceed to delineate a candidate for the *trace* or stored *representation* in connection with such a case of remembering what happened? Events, occasions, scenes, images, do not come to us pre-identified and captioned, parcelled up into recognisably discrete units with their associated conceptualis-ations emanating from them. We have no *context-independent, uniform criteria* for delineating an 'event' as a discrete unitary piece of the world, nor for recognising an 'occasion's' boundaries, nor a 'scene's' salient features apart from *context and purpose*, no matter what it is we are calling an event, occasion or scene. Did I 'store' a 'trace' of 'the students', or of the students-and-their-milling-around-looking-for-seats, or of the beginning-of-the-class, or of the-disruption-caused-by-the-explosion, in a succession of 'discrete' episodes, or did I 'store' the 'whole occasion'? If the latter, how did I bound it? When did *it* begin? If I think hard enough I might be able to recollect some details of events which *preceded* the occasion now being recounted. Does this mean that I had stored that separately, or just that I had 'started the account' at the point when and where the retrieval mechanism made the (much longer) 'stored representation' available to me? The point is, of course, that a recollection is available *in the first instance* as an undefeated account or narrative, and as such its 'boundedness' as well as its 'salient features' are *always relative to some purposes of telling*, of recounting, on some occasion. 'Thoroughness' and 'completeness' are essentially functions of situated criteria and practical purposes here. Ralph Gerard advances the following claim:

> Some tests of perception suggest that each tenth of a second is a single 'frame' of human experience for the human brain. In that tenth of a second it can receive perhaps a thousand units of information, called bits. In 70 years, not allowing for any reception during sleep, some 15 trillion bits might pour into the brain and perhaps be stored there. Since this number is 1,000 times larger than the total of nerve cells, the problem of storage is not exactly simple.[9]

We are not told, however, what counts as a 'unit of information' here, and how any such claim could be tested. Our historicity in the world is not readily decomposable into 'units' independent of some orientation to relevances of various (perhaps generically inconsistent) sorts. I can recollect many discrete words in French (although, since I *speak/know* English it would be odd to say of me that I (can) 'recollect' or 'remember' *English* words or their meanings[10]), and here one may perhaps want to say that I somehow 'stored' (a representation of) the words in my brain; but when it comes to my recollecting *situations* (events, occasions, encounters, etc.) the problem of the 'unit' becomes more transparently hard to define and encapsulate in any non-arbitrary way independent of some purpose *in telling about them*. The chief reason why much of the empirical work on human memory capacities has been done on (lists of) words, (series of) numbers and other phenomena such as arrays of objects is precisely to avoid the problem of the individuation of memories, which is the first logical step for storage hypotheses. Just as Wittgenstein came to realise that his doctrines in the *Tractatus* arbitrarily assumed *absolute* notions of 'simple' and 'complex', so must we realise that theorists who espouse trace-storage models of occurrent remembering (frequently) assume *absolute* notions of 'the whole of what was remembered' and 'part of what was remembered', failing to notice that any concretisation of either may be interchangeably described depending upon the purposes of the telling. They tend to reify 'components' of what is manifested in a recollection as enduring properties of persons rather than as contextually variable aspects of a telling's construction.

Because we know what it is to 'store a unit of information in a memory-bank or address' in a computer, we may think that we are on the way to revealing the principles of memory-storage in human beings (and perhaps some species of animals). But when we remember a word, an event or situation, we are not thereby remembering a 'unit of information' in the computer scientist's sense of 'information' (e.g., after Shannon and Weaver). What we say (if corroborated or ratifiable) shows what we remember when what we remember is such as to require the use of language for its manifestation, but we are not thereby to be construed as 'translating our stored neural information into (English) words and sentences, phrases and narratives'. How could I tell, to what criteria could I appeal, if someone were to ask how I knew which neural 'bit' corresponded to which 'bit' of the recollection or 'aspect' of the events being recollected on some occasion? Does the neurally encoded 'bit' of information simply translate *itself* into words and issue forth from my mouth correctly when my recollections are expressed in words and ratified as such? The incoherences we face here are the product of a muddled notion of 'storage'.

Consider the following hypothesis: memory capacities depend upon protein syntheses for 'storage' or 'memorial represen-tation', or, in its stronger form, a memory is stored as protein or RNA.[11] Such an hypothesis might be conceivable if some criteria could be developed for the individuation of 'a memory' so that its description might be mapped onto a protein chain or sequence of molecules (or a sequence of molecular *transformations*). Although retention difficulties following learning trials are reported in some animals when protein synthesis is impaired,[12] this cannot show the nature of the relationship between recalling (or *not* forgetting) and protein synthesis to consist in the *embodiment* of what is recalled *in* the protein. In the case of animals, the recalling or remembering is necessarily a remembering *how to*, the retention of an ability, capacity, skill in bringing off some performance(s), and not in any remembering *that*, or 'propositional, discursive' remembering. And, as we have argued, an ability, capacity or skill may be facilitated by, but hardly *stored in*, any specific organic or biochemical structure.

Kenny[13] and Baker and Hacker[14] have recently attacked the fallacy of 'vehicle-reductionism', whereby some ability or power is analysed into the structure of some 'vehicle' which may account for the ability:

> Whisky can intoxicate. The vehicle of its ability is the alcohol it contains, but the alcohol is not identical with the intoxicating power. One can weigh the alcohol, but not the ability to intoxicate. If an ability is distinct from its vehicle, *a fortiori* it is distinct from the structure of its vehicle which may explain the ability.[15]

The literal identification of mental abilities such as forms of remembering with neural states or structures or biochemical components of such states or structures is but a form of illegitimate 'vehicle-reductionism'. The hypothesis formulated as 'memories *are* protein syntheses' is only rational if we allow that a remembering-how or a remembering-that (an ability and an occurrence respectively) are reducible to the structures of their vehicles (persons with brains). Since we cannot allow that order of identification on logical grounds, the hypothesis is incoherent. Our brains and their chemical constituents enable us to remember things, how to do things, and the rest of our memory-related achievements, but they do not *house* what they enable us to do and achieve. My (discursively manifested) memories are *of* something, *about* something, *that* something was the case, etc. Having certain proteins in my brain may enable me to remember (to have the memory of) something, but cannot itself *be* the memory of something. I cannot even see how it could be imagined that a correct *account of the past* (for which extensionally equivalent alternative accounts may be given, and between which *none* may be considered *the only real account*) might be contained in a protein or protein synthesis.

Let us suppose that someone were to concede the argument so far, and that he were to say: 'Just demonstrating that *available* theoretical formulations are subject to the sort of deficiencies you claim they suffer from is not the same as showing that *no* theoretical account of "storage" is logically possible.' Malcolm, however, has tried to argue exactly this in his very significant work on memory and mind.[16] However, I think that his discussion of the problem of storage in the chapter 'Retention and Storage' is ultimately unconvincing. For Malcolm, *retention*, which is implicated in memory, does not entail *storage* of what is retained. He argues along the following sort of lines:

One might say of a woman whom one has not seen for several years that she retains her good looks. One would mean that she was previously good-looking and still is. There would be no implication that her good looks are in storage. It might be said of a man that despite the many hardships he has suffered he retains a sunny disposition. Has his sunny disposition been stored?[17]

Of course, as Malcolm notes, it is *sometimes* legitimate to link storage with retention, as when someone says that he has retained some object of (e.g.,) furniture, from which it may be inferred that it is stored somewhere (especially if the speaker is known to be moving into a new apartment and is not yet there: we do not say we are 'storing' furniture currently *in use*.) Malcolm claims from here that 'To take the storage metaphors . . . as giving some warrant to the assumption of *traces* (*literal* storage) is both humorous and saddening . . . . The confusion of the idea of retention with the idea of literal storage is conspicuous in the writings of theorists and researchers in the neuropsychology of memory.'[18]

Taking the possibility of *some* notion of 'literal' storage seriously does not entail taking any *available* theoretical formulation about 'storage' as adequate. Although we might *not* intelligibly be spoken of as 'storing information' in one sense, we may well be engaged in 'storing information' *by virtue of the fact that* neuronal or synaptic or glial cell changes in my brain enable me to recall various sorts of 'information' (such as your name if I know it and can produce it if asked to 'recall, remember or bring it to mind'). The problem with Malcolm's account is that he nowhere specifies the logical structure of a theoretical scheme appropriate for stating *any* relationship of brain states/functions to the capacity to recall and remember things, names, events, scenes, situations and so on. Indeed, he does not tell us *what* role he would assign to neurophysiology in the pursuit of scientific knowledge of memory.

A very widely held view (from Lashley[19] to McConnell[20] and John[21], amongst many others) is that memory is a 'matter of multiple representations in the brain',[22] even though 'Few principles concerning the structural representation of memories may be described as well established.'[23] Anderson and Bower[24] describe their well-known experimental findings about rememberings of certain kinds in terms of computer-analogical constructions like internal 'binary codes' – reminiscent of Jerry Fodor's 'organic' realisation of something functioning as a machine-code does in actual computers, only here subserving 'memory capacities'. Krech, in a valuable overview,[25] criticised the 'insularity' of scientists trained in neurochemistry, and noted the opinion that few real advances have been made in research on brain biochemistry in connection with memory functions and their neurological facilitators. It is interesting and significant for our purposes that Krech advises psychobiologists and brain biochemists, from a standpoint of colleagiality and common interest in the study of memory, to: 'Go constantly to look at memory in people. Know what you are studying, and whence came your question.'[26] Although many times I have heard it asserted that James McConnell's work on planarian worms and rats and the associated neuronal RNA-levels implicated in their learning has effectively shown that 'memories are chemically encoded', it is not at all clear to me how best to interpret McConnell's findings. There have been many suggestions about factors *other than* 'chemical memory transfer' for the increased light-sensitivity of worms who had cannibalised parts of worms trained to avoid light.[27] As for the claim (or hypothesis) that the learning of specific tasks by rats increased in speed following an injection into their brains of brain extracts from previously trained rats[28], this might clearly be interpreted (although perhaps wrongly if more evidence arrives) as a matter of overall cortical transformation which turns out to subserve more rapid learning of *any* task. In any event, *if* some specific ability (at some task) is facilitated by the formation of some chemical or neuronal *brain structure(s)*, we are exclusively in the domain of remembering-how-to (especially in the worm, rat and cat cases, which are the only ones studied) and *not* in the domain of (propositional, discursive, concept-mediated) remembering-*that*. And it is for the latter (episodic, occurrent, usually linguistically-available) class of rememberings that the notion of *storage of information* was designed, *not* for the former. Nothing need be 'represented internally', since you cannot 'represent' an ability or a capacity in anything, and nothing need be literally stored, either, since you cannot *store* an ability, capacity or knowledge-*how*-to. Why are we being told to think of the chemical elements McConnell may have isolated as 'encodings of information', as 'memorial representations', 'engrams' or 'internal (neurophysiological) representations'? Why not think of them just as part of the biochemical facilitators for the exercise of certain (specific) *capacities*? 'Memory' need hardly come into the interpretation. Where it does, it does so in the most anaemic sense as 'having learned-how-to' and (still) 'being able-to' (i.e., still having the ability). As Munsat has remarked, 'not everything that one can know can be spoken of as being remembered'.[29]

There is absolutely *no* evidence available which really bears upon the issue of propositional (linguistic-conceptual), image-laden, 'sudden' or not-sudden but occurrent remembering, and its relationship to (claimed) biochemical storage-vehicles.[30] There are, however, claims made about the sudden occurrence of recollections by persons of various events, scenes, experiences, etc. at the onset of electrode stimulation of parts of the amygdala, temporal lobe and other neural sites.[31] Malcolm's[32] and Valenstein's[33] critical re-appraisals of these neurophysiological experiments and their findings leave us without much confidence in their adequacy, however. And it is still radically unclear exactly what theoretical inferences were to be made from them. (It is also unclear where Malcolm and Valenstein think brain-behaviour studies should go.)

One of the major stumbling blocks to the formulation of an adequate explanation-scheme for the neurophysiology/biochemistry of memory, to be completed with the empirical details unearthed by research, is the following. We must try to explain sudden rememberings, and their putative neurological pre-conditions. It is virtually impossible to think of any warrantable criteria for *individuating* (conceptualised) percepts and other experiences into items, elements, components or even wholes which are (supposed to be) registered in 'traces', 'engrams', 'stored *representations*' and so forth. Individuations of events, experiences, scenes and occasions, as well as actions, utterances and other 'intelligibilia', are routinely accomplished by practical speakers for specific occasions, audiences and purposes. There are *no* decontextualisable standards or criteria for otherwise individuating 'what happened', 'what was said', 'who did what', 'when it occurred' and the rest of the possible object-complements for expressions such as: 'I (just) remembered —'.

I do not think that any argument with which I am familiar in the philosophy of mind, and in work on what I have called 'the social construction of mind',[34] has shaken my faith in the correctness of *some* (as yet untold) story about recall and its neuro-chemical or physiological enabler(s). Nonetheless, the problem of warrantably chosen 'units of analysis' still looms large. Some considerable distance may be travelled if it is more widely appreciated that theoretically adequate characterisations of our research problems depend upon conceptual (and ethnomethodo-logical) elucidations of everyday remembering, everyday memory-claims, everyday forgettings, etc. and their logic of orderliness as 'forms of life'.[35] We need – not more experi-mentation alone, but – *clarifications* of our phenomena as, in the first instance, mundanely available matters. Specific theories of 'traces', 'engrams' and 'stored representations' nearly all beg huge questions about retrieval, the individuation of 'what is remembered (represented)', *corresponding* individuations of (hypo-thetical) brain sites (e.g., neurons, proteins, *sets* of either, *changes* in either, etc., etc.), and the theoretical role played by any such neural item in the whole picture of human occurrent and dispo-sitional rememberings. Be this as it may, I believe (*pace* Malcolm) that a wholesale rejection of a neurophysiological theory of storage-facilitation in *any* form is quite unwarranted. Some (perhaps most extant) such theories do indeed suffer from the sort of logical maladies by which Malcolm accuses them of being afflicted: but it is significant (at least to me) that Malcolm's other-wise incisive argumentation fails him when he rejects as logically inappropriate *all* talk of storage in relation to remembering. If I suddenly remember yesterday's newspaper headline, and can quote it correctly, I may certainly be said to have stored it, and there is one sense in which this may be *literally* taken: there may be something *specific* about my CNS, brain biochemistry and/or brain functioning which enabled me to come up with *it, now*.[36] And the question: *what* specific something(s)? is not a product of confusion but a way of beginning to decipher a *genuine* mystery of nature. My point here, however, is that the elucidation of memory as a feature of the public praxis of social life is a pre-requisite for the proper articulation of relevant questions addressed to the study of the nervous system.

NOTES

1. Stanley Munsat, *The Concept of Memory* (New York: Random House, 1967).

2. Norman Malcolm, *Memory and Mind* (Ithaca, New York and London: Cornell University Press, 1977).

3. Ibid., p. 224.

4. Les Holborow, 'The "Prejudice" in Favor of Psychophysical Parallelism' in Godfrey Vesey (ed.), *Understanding Wittgenstein: The Royal Institute of Philosophy Lectures, vol. 7 (1972–73)* (London: Macmillan, 1974) p. 202. See also Roger Squires, 'Memory Unchained', *Philosophical Review*, vol. 78, April 1969.

5. J.F.M. Hunter, 'Wittgenstein and Materialism', *Mind*, vol. 86, no. 344, October 1977, p. 528.

6. Ibid.

7. Ibid., p. 529. Hunter concludes by proposing that 'whatever exactly we might one day explain neurologically it would not be remembering. Something's not being hearsay or inference, or the speaker's being a witness, do not call for a neurological explanation, if they call for any at all.' (p. 531). He characterises this as a 'mild' suggestion. (Ibid.). A much fuller elaboration of the 'facts' about memory which we might attempt to explain neurophysiologically is necessary to support this claim, which might of course be true.

8. W.F. Brewer, 'The Problem of Meaning and Higher Mental Processes' in W.B. Weimer and D.S. Palermo (eds), *Cognition and the Symbolic Processes* (New York: LEA/John Wiley, 1974) p. 284. His references are to I. Begg and A. Paivio, 'Concreteness and Imagery in Sentence Meaning', *Journal of Verbal Learning and Verbal Behavior*, vol. 8, 1969, and to W.F. Brewer, 'Memory for Ideas: Synonym Substitutions', unpublished MSS, University of Illinois, 1974. I have added italics to the quotation in the text.

9. Ralph W. Gerard, 'What is Memory?' in *Psychobiology* (San Francisco: Scientific American: W.H. Freeman, 1967) p. 126.

10. I am grateful to W.T. Anderson for this observation.

11. See Norman E. Spear, *The Processing of Memories: Forgetting and Retention* (New York: LEA/John Wiley, 1978), p. 333, *et seq*. See also D.A. Booth, 'Protein Synthesis and Memory' in J.A. Deutsch (ed.), *The Physiological Basis of Memory* (New York: Academic Press: 1973) pp. 27–58. But how could one 'decode' from a protein chain into a narrative account or image of a past event?

12. Spear, *Memories*, pp. 335–39.

13. A.J.P. Kenny, *Will, Freedom and Power* (Oxford: Blackwell, 1976) p. 10.

14. G.P. Baker and P.M.S. Hacker, *Wittgenstein: Understanding and Meaning*, vol. 1, (Oxford: University of Chicago Press/Blackwell, 1980).

15. Ibid., p. 611. Their entire discussion of 'Understanding and Ability' (pp. 595–620) is immensely clarifying.

16. Malcolm, *Memory and Mind*.

17. Ibid., p. 197.

18. Ibid., p. 199.

19. K.S. Lashley, 'In Search of the Engram', *Symposia of the Society for Experimental Biology*, vol. 4 (Washington D.C.: 1950) pp. 454–582.

20. J.V. McConnell, T. Shigehisha and H. Salive, 'Attempts to Transfer

Approach and Avoidance Responses by RNA Injection in Rats', *Journal of Biological Psychology*, vol. 10, no. 2, pp. 32–50.

21. E.R. John, *Mechanisms of Memory* (New York: Academic Press, 1967).

22. Spear, *Memories*, p. 42.

23. Ibid., p. 43.

24. J.R. Anderson and G.H. Bower, *Human Associative Memory* (Washington, D.C.: Hemisphere, 1974).

25. D. Krech, 'Discussion' in J.L. McGough (ed.), *Advances in Behavioral Biology*, vol. 4: *The Chemistry of Mood, Motivation and Memory* (New York: Plenum Press, 1972).

26. Ibid., p. 223. (Quoted in Spear, *Memories*, p. 10).

27. See, e.g., Georges Chapouthier, 'Behavioral Studies of the Molecular Basis of Memory' in Deutsch, *Physiological Basis of Memory*.

28. See note (20) *supra*.

29. Munsat, *Concept of Memory*, p. xv.

30. See, e.g., H.A. Bursen, *Dismantling the Memory Machine: A Philosophical Investigation of Machine Theories of Memory* (Dordrecht: Reidel, 1978); Spear, *Memories*, *passim*, and Derek Richter (ed.), *Aspects of Learning and Memory* (New York: Basic Books, 1966).

31. For a fuller discussion of these experiments (by Penfield and others), see Leonard A. Stevens, *Explorers of the Brain* (New York: Knopf, 1971).

32. Malcolm, *Memory and Mind*, ch. 10.

33. Elliot S. Valenstein, *Brain Control: A Critical Examination of Brain Stimulation and Psychosurgery* (New York: John Wiley, 1973).

34. J. Coulter, *The Social Construction of Mind* (London: Macmillan, 1978).

35. Perhaps in a broader sense than in Wittgenstein's (original) uses of the expression. See J.F.M. Hunter, ' "Forms of Life" in Wittgenstein's *Philosophical Investigations*' in E.D. Klemke (ed.), *Essays on Wittgenstein* (Urbana: University of Illinois, 1971).

36. At present, the likeliest candidate is some molecular transformation in the cortex. However, even in the (unlikely) event that such a specific transformation occurs and is discovered, the problem of *how* it enables something specific to be remembered (in conduct) is an altogether different order of problem.

5 On sentient automata theory

A unifying metaphysical theme underlying various forms of cognitive theorising is the conception of human agents as *sentient automata*. Persons are conceived of as complex mechanisms (or sets of inter-related mechanisms) each of which has some deterministic function pertaining to any form of human conduct. Neurophysiological events and processes (albeit under 'mentalistic' descriptions) are theoretically invokable in accounting not only for involuntary bodily movements but for the entire gamut of activities involving the human agent. The study of human beings under the auspices of such a conception may be termed *sentient automata theory construction*.

Dennett is quite unequivocal in embracing sentient automata theory in his claim that 'the open question now is not whether mechanistic explanation of human motion [sic] is possible, but just whether it will ultimately have crucial gaps of randomness (like the indeterminists' mechanistic explanation of electrons) or not (like the mechanistic explanation of macroscopic systems such as motors and billiard tables)'.[1] He proceeds to assume the possibility of a cybernetician or neurophysiologist handing us volumes of fine print comprising the 'design of this man's behavioral control system'[2] – encompassing behaviour both 'rational' and 'versatile'.[3] Weil also recommends the goal of a unified mechanistic account of all human conduct utilising the 'concepts and terms of neurophysiology'.[4] Many others concur with such a recommendation.

It might at first appear somewhat idle and premature to set out to examine the assumptions of such a programme, especially since it is clear that neither neurophysiology nor any related discipline is within sight of delivering orders of information about the functioning of the cortex which might be brought to bear upon such arguments as have recently been advanced. However, so much present-day research effort and theoretical argument in the human sciences depends upon the cogency of sentient automata theory in general that it is worthwhile considering the matter here. And the discussion does, I think, bring into sharp focus various interesting contemporary ways in which some quite classical metaphysical issues about human agency are being formulated and treated.

1 AN ELEMENTARY PARADOX OF SENTIENT AUTOMATA THEORY

John Thorp, in his recent book *Free Will*,[5] states the fundamental obstacle facing sentient automata theory (conceived of by him in terms of neurophysiological determinism) as follows:

> [E]ither we are free and therefore nature is not deterministic, or nature is deterministic and therefore we are not free. The consequent of each of these horns imports embarrassment; for on the one hand we are, for certain reasons, inclined to believe that nature is deterministic, and on the other hand we do suppose ourselves free, and some of our moral and legal institutions seem to depend upon that supposition.[6]

As parts of the natural, physical world, as organisms, we participate nonetheless as 'free, rational agents' in our mundane affairs. In many, if not all, circumstances it makes sense to conceive of ourselves as free beings; yet as physical organisms our nervous systems are supposed to be subject to laws of nature. How are these apparently irreconcilable claims to be dealt with? *If* neurophysiological states and events could intelligibly be said to *determine all our behaviour*, at every or any level of its description, then since such states and events are to be formulated mechanistically in terms of causal relations this must entail, were the proposal sound, that all of our conduct is amenable to automatistic explanation and to that extent transcends our claims to free autonomous agency in the most radical way. As Thorp notes, 'a deterministic neurophysiological explanation renders its explanandum as naturally necessary, as something which under the laws of nature *had* to happen.'[7] This would contradict the claim to freedom of action which logically entails the possibility that an agent *could have done otherwise*.

Thorp sets out to defend 'libertarianism' against the threat of what I am here calling sentient automata theorising by arguing for *agent causality* as a basic, primitive and unanalysable notion *alongside*, rather than decomposable into, *event* causality. This is not the place to track down his ingenious arguments, nor to assess the many difficulties he faces in securing his case. Nonetheless, he is right in facing up to and treating an oft-heard pseudo-defence of the concept of freedom of action, namely, the invocation of *indeterminism* in neurophysiological events. It is a commonplace that classical mechanical determinism in physics cannot handle various quantum phenomena, and it appears to be the case that the central nervous system in man exhibits similar indeterminacies in its functioning. Some libertarians have sought to locate the operation of agent causality in the interstices of CNS events (such as neuronal firings) by arguing from the presence of some degree of *randomness* in CNS events to the freedom of the agent. Thorp asks how persons manage to organise their free actions and decisions so that they occur simultaneously with unpredictable transformations in the brain. There is a clear conceptual difference between mere randomness and genuine freedom of action and decision.[8] He goes on to remark that we are not nearer freedom with *random* neural events than we were with causally determined ones:

> if our decisions are what they are because by pure chance a neuron fired sooner rather than later, then the responsibility for that decision is to be laid at the feet of that undetermined physical event: we are delivered out of the bondage of causal determinism only to find ourselves in the bondage of randomness.[9]

Neither determinism nor indeterminism in the operation of our CNS appears compatible with the rational assignation of freedom and responsibility to an agent's actions. We shall confine ourselves here to a consideration of mechanistic-deterministic versions of sentient automata theorising, although not foreclosing upon the issues raised by genuine indeterminacies in neural functioning. If we are able to specify some respects in which the strong version may be faulted, then perhaps they may be extended to the weak (indeterministic) version as well. We shall see.

2 DO NEURAL EVENTS CAUSE ME TO 'DO WHAT I DO'?

The converse of this question is often encountered: do I cause my neuronal firings to activate what I do, enable me to do whatever it is I do? And, if so, how do I bring this about? I think that questions such as these have a clear bearing upon the search for some solution to the fundamental paradox here under review: the contradiction, or seeming contradiction, between saying that I am responsible for my actions which I perform freely and saying that neuronal events, of which I know nothing and which operate wholly out of my awareness, make them happen – thereby obliterating the distinction between my being responsible and my not being responsible. If my conduct is, all of a piece, the *output* of impersonal, naturally occurring physico-chemical-electrical events without any intervention by an 'agent', then the applicability of concepts like 'personal responsibility' and 'moral accountability' becomes problematic; they only *seem* to apply to me.

What could it mean, however, to claim that 'I bring it about that' my neurons fire in such a way that I am thereby enabled to do what I (choose to) do? If 'bringing it about that my neurons fire' is a description of some mysterious kind of *activity* which *I* perform (or the *upshot* of some sort of personal 'activity'), it is certainly not something which I am ever aware of engaging in, nor is it something I would know how to do if I were given an order to do it. And yet we feel impelled to recognise some kind of difference between a case in which, say, my neurons just happened to fire in a certain pattern, thereby causing some involuntary bodily movement to occur, and a case in which my neurons' firing enabled me to undertake some movement or action which may be described as 'voluntary', 'chosen', 'deliberate' or 'planned'.

It is in encountering apparent paradoxes such as these that many philosophers, psychologists and neurophysiological theorists have invoked a notion of agency as something other than a 'person', as something transcending natural necessity and causal law: a 'will', a 'mind', a 'self', and so forth. Chisholm has remarked upon such a theoretical propensity as follows:

> [We use] such terms as 'active power', 'the autonomy of the will', 'prime mover', or 'higher levels of causality' – terms designating something to which we apparently need not refer when expressing the conclusions of physics and the natural sciences. But I believe we cannot know whether such theories enable us to escape our dilemma. For it seems impossible to conceive what the relation is that, according to these theories, holds between the 'will', 'self', 'mover' or 'active power', on the one hand, and the bodily events this power is supposed to control, on the other – the relation between the 'activities' of the self and the events described by physics [or by neuro-physiological inquiry – JC].[10]

Thorp valiantly tries to come to terms with this sort of difficulty, but finds himself locked into a scheme in which mystery is piled upon mystery:

> The libertarian, then, is proposing a kind of causality which is not capable of being analysed into our normal kind of causality, event causality. It may seem that he is thereby wantonly introducing mystery into the world. I think that this charge is correct, but perhaps it can be rendered less

damaging by the following anodyne consideration. He is not so much introducing mystery into the world as introducing more mystery into the world: the event causality with which we seem so comfortable is itself unfathomably mysterious.'[11]

Postulating an 'active power' irreducible to (neurophysiological event-) causality, Thorp finds himself construing central nervous system functions as inhabited by a *deus ex machina*. His task is to persuade a late twentieth-century audience, presumably comfortable with ordinary notions of causation, to accept such a notion, and his approach in handling this problem is to try to naturalise the 'mystery'. It is a superb effort; too often proponents of either sentient automata theory or libertarianism in its radical form simply avoid the issue. But Thorp's notion of an 'active power'[12] is just too vague to settle the matter.

Having said all this, we should nonetheless take seriously a common candidate for this neurological 'mover', the 'will'.

3 NEUROPHYSIOLOGICAL 'ACTS OF VOLITION'

Although it is rare to find philosophers and behavioural scientists arguing that the 'mind' is an entity or object in a mysterious 'space' apart from the brain but which nonetheless acts upon the brain and causes it to work in the ways it does, the concept of the 'will' may appear more recalcitrantly suited to fit this bill. (I confess to finding it odd that Sir John Eccles should still, after Wittgenstein, Ryle and Malcolm, invoke 'mind' and 'self' as entities in a trialistic ontological scheme in which they function as determinants of brain processes.[13])

It was Wittgenstein who raised the question of the 'will' as any sort of *entity* at all in his astute observations on the topic. And it was Ryle who effectively dispelled the notion that every action requires a prior act of will, noting that it was an infinite-regress argument and thus fallacious. However, they were not obviously thinking of neurophysiological matters when they ruled out 'willing' as an omnipresent phenomenon prior to action. Could the notion be given such a sense? Only if we arbitrarily reconstrue its meaning so as to fit our theoretical requirements. And yet such a notion is, as Thorp so rightly notices, embodied in many anatomy and physiology texts: it is invoked at points where some organ or muscle is characterised as 'subject to the will' or to 'conscious control', or where a muscle or muscular-nervous concatenation is described as 'voluntary', as enabling 'voluntary movement'. 'The beating of the heart is not subject to the will, but the opening and closing of the epiglottis is.'[14] Thorp goes on to note that 'what the physiology of this being "subject to the will" amounts to is generally described, darkly, as being controlled by "higher centres of the brain" ',[15] but again contradicts his earlier stipulations about 'freedom' as freedom from event-causation (either inner or outer) when he remarks that such a view of the *control* by higher centres of the brain 'is true'.[16]

Let us suppose that we could understand the expression 'subject to the will' in a less objectified way as 'subject to acts of volition'. The question now becomes: what is an 'act of volition'? Wittgenstein clearly thought the question utterly spurious, as in his remarks in *Philosophical Investigations*:

> 621. Let us not forget this: when 'I raise my arm', my arm goes up. And the problem arises: what is left over if I subtract the fact that my arm goes up from the fact that I raise my arm?
> ((Are the kinaesthetic sensations my willing?))
> 622. When I raise my arm I do not usually *try* to raise it.[17]

In latter-day accounts, acts of volition are imputed to brains or parts of brains in order to attempt to come to terms with the distinction we normally make between actions undertaken voluntarily and movements made involuntarily, between conscious, rational activities and mere reflexes and spasms, etc. Yet no such account with which I am familiar comes to grips with the very same problem of the initiation of an 'act of volition', however biologised our description has become (theoretically speaking). Such a Primary Impulse will either be subject to the same (metaphysical) speculative question as to *its* initiation out-side a causal or random system, or it will be assimilated to impersonal, causal processes of law-governed kinds (or of probabilistic construction), once again regressing into a domain beyond free interception or agency, beyond human *fiat*. Wittgen-stein seemed to have considered the question of the initiation of human actions as inappropriate for physiology and psychology as scientific disciplines, and as one which has a vernacular meaning only in certain circumstances and for certain purposes. There is also some indication from his remarks in *Zettel* that he eschewed physiological-deterministic 'explanations' for other orders of phenomena for which present-day neuroscientific theory is being developed (e.g., in sentient-automata-theoretic models). For example, he declares, in connection with a comment upon retinal-image inversion:

> But must there be a physiological explanation here? Why don't we just leave explaining alone? – But you would never talk like that, if you were examining the behaviour of a machine – Well, who says that a living creature, an animal body, is a machine in this sense? (*Zettel*, para. 614).

Here it appears as though Wittgenstein is simply setting his face against then-fashionable versions of sentient-automata thinking about human beings, and that he does so without detailed argument. Indeed, his opinion or judgment here is that we tend to become beguiled by wholly inappropriate models, pictures, *Vorstellungen*, paradigms and analogies to the point where, in the midst of our misassimilations (e.g., of humans to automata or to beings functioning as automata), we encounter conceptual anomalies. The most we could *ever* say of a robot or android of human design and manufacture was that it could *simulate* voluntary activity, that it *could appear to be* free, rational and conscious, that it might *act as if* it were capable of free choice (rather than programmed determinations or programmed probabilistic selections based on a randomising unit).

Of course, Wittgenstein was not concerning himself with

exactly the same problems as ours, was not seeking to contribute
to the metatheory of behavioural science research, but his insights
in these areas strike me as wholly salient. In large measure, the
notion of a neurophysiological act of will or volition is a transposition into physiological-psychological theorising and speculative model-construction of a notion of willings as mental acts long
discredited in the twentieth-century philosophy of mind in
Wittgenstein's tradition. All the familiar difficulties attend the
notion of a *neurophysiological* 'volition' as an antecedent to a human
action considered free, as attended the mentalistic notion.

4 PROBLEMS WITH 'COMPATIBILISM'

One familiar attempt to get out of the maze in which we are lost is
to invoke a distinction between a 'behavioural event' and a full-
blown 'action', and to observe that the same behavioural event(s)
under different circumstances amount to different sorts of actions,
and that different behavioural events under different circumstances amount to the same action. This takes stock of the fact
that there is no one-to-one mapping of action-predicates onto
descriptions of bodily motions. Since neural impulses 'determine'
the movements of our muscles and other physiological equipment, it could be argued that a neurophysiological-determinist
account is logically appropriate for behavioural events (e.g.,
bodily movements) which enter into the depiction of actions, but
that for actions themselves some other order of explanation is
appropriate, one that invokes 'reasons' for acting and which
accommodates the conceptual apparatus of 'freedom', 'responsibility', 'intentionality' and the rest. Thus, since 'actions' are
logically irreducible to 'behavioural events' *per se*, CNS events
cannot be invoked to explain them adequately. Only 'reasons'
and 'rules' can explain human actions *qua* actions.

There are several moves which have been made to counter this
story, and I shall discuss one of the most significant of these before
outlining my own version of the topic. It is concerned with the
nature of 'reasons', such as having a desire to do something or

having an intention to do something. Why not construe these states of affairs as 'states of the organism'? Weil, for example, believes that Malcolm failed to prove that 'desirings and intendings must fall outside the set of neurophysiological conditions which are causally sufficient for some particular piece of behavior'[18] – presumably of the rational and/or versatile sort for which desire/intention talk is appropriate *prima facie*. Yet both 'desiring' and 'intending' are predicates whose logical powers have been explored by conceptual analysts on many occasions, and it is clear that they do not have either a sense or reference which is decomposable into discrete states or processes *of* (or *in*) the body, even though all sorts of states and processes may be going on in recipients of such (rationally made) ascriptions all or most of the time. My desiring something may be an enduringly describable state *of affairs* about me, exhibited in and instantiated in all sorts of ways – through my talk, my other (non-locutionary) activities, my dispositions, my circumstances – but it is not an observable state of my body to which neurological antecedents may be 'regularly associated', as Weil would have it. It may correctly be said of me while I am asleep that I desire one day to be wealthy, without such a predication being based upon any determination of an organic state. My desiring water, on the other hand, may well be based upon a physiological condition available as a clock-timeable state of my body, but the state of my body is not itself the 'desiring', only the grounds for the desiring. The broad range of situations within which desiring is rationally avowable by or ascribable to me is such as to preclude any codification of constants remotely relevant to a biological story. A similar line of argument can be advanced for my intending to do or not to do any of a vast range of things. Neither 'desiring' nor 'intending' are descriptions of or concepts for *states* of a person, although they might be thought of as parts of a description of some state *of affairs*, in which reference to contextual particulars is either explicit or implicit. This candidate for compatibilism – locating 'reasons' such as desires and intentions as states for which neurological antecendents might be forthcoming – simply will not work. (Wittgenstein once asked a pointed question, which ought to embarrass any proponent of the intention-having-is-a-state account, in the following: ' "I have the intention of going away tomorrow." – When have you that intention? The whole time; or intermittently?'[19]).

One line of defence for *compatibilist* versions of 'intentionalist' and 'mechanistic' explanations of human doings consists in various elaborations of a fundamental claim: that 'actions', unlike mere organic movements, are *rule-governed*, whereas the component parts may well be *law-governed*. In such an account, the notion of governance by rules *must* be taken to mean that human actions are quite literally the output of some internalised programme, such as is envisaged by cognitivist models of the sort we have already discussed. Although there is some merit to the suggestion that actions and the reasons for them are related together grammatically rather than deterministically, this particular conception needs to be understood, not as support for an 'internal-program' model of action and cognition, but as a (somewhat loose) way of taking stock of the fact that in producing and assessing 'reasons for actions', we employ distinctions which presuppose some 'standards' of intelligibility, rationality and morality, as when we say of someone's reason for some action that it was 'a good reason' or 'a poor excuse', that it was 'appropriate' or 'inappropriate', that it was 'sensible' or 'eccentric', etc. Not any old utterance, however grammatically formed, can *count* as a reason for some action unless circumstantially-bound criteria are satisfied. In these ways, we want to say that the ties between reasons and actions, and the describability of actions and reasons in the first instance, are subject to assessment in terms of standards or 'rules'. We are *not* thereby committing ourselves to a version of actions as the output of some programmed system of instructions operative out of awareness. It is, as I have already noted, somewhat strained to speak even of a computer as a 'rule-following' device just in virtue of its programming. Properly to be engaged in following a rule, as distinct from *analogically* to be engaged in rule-following, entails a variety of possibilities alien to computers. These include the possibility of checking back to see if the rule applies where one had thought that it did, of reformulating a rule so as to fit a recalcitrant case or instance or situation, of reconceiving of the nature of any such case or instance so as to fit the terms of the rule already settled in advance, and so on. Although perhaps some day a computer might be made which operates in ways similar to these distinctively human capacities, it is clearly in a strained sense that we would want to insist (for other than economy of speech) that computational artefacts are rule-following devices. In any event, most of our activities are better thought of as in-accord-with rules or standards; only in certain cases and in certain contexts is it right to speak of an action as the outcome of *following* a rule. The 'behaviour' of a computer is *invariantly* (when running properly) the output of program-governance. Moreover, among people some rule may be said to have been broken by them; for computers, there is no rule-*breaking* – only malfunctioning.[20] Thus, invoking computers as existence-proofs for mechanically functioning entities which perform in ways describable as rule-following cannot suffice to buttress compatibilism.[21]

What, then, ought we to conclude about compatibilist versions of the brain/behaviour problem? As I understand their point, compatibilist versions are designed to reconcile one part of our conceptual scheme with another: brains construed as law-governed entities consisting of components whose operations are describable as causing what we do, and persons construed as intention-forming beings subject to predicates such as 'free', 'responsible', 'rational', 'moral' and so on. The compatibilist wants to have his cake and eat it too, and yet he is *already* making a theoretical concession to mechanism which constantly threatens to undermine his putative acceptance of a conceptual framework within which freedom of action has a place, along with the range of predicates appropriate to rational, moral and discursive conduct. However, in order to make these distinctive orders of conceptualisation of human behaviour sit together in a comprehensive theoretical scheme, the compatibilist must reformulate our ordinary concepts of 'reasons' and 'rules or conduct' by reifying them into internal states of the CNS or by treating them as epiphenomenal to the *basic* neurophysiological picture. Both moves appear to me to be unworkable.

5 DENNETT'S PROPOSED RECONCILIATION OF (INDETERMINISTIC) MECHANISM WITH WHAT LIBERTARIANS 'SAY THEY WANT'

Dennett, in the course of a discussion touched off by a well-known **paper** by Wiggins entitled 'Towards a Reasonable Libertarianism'[22], advances the following proposal:[23]

> when we are faced with an important decision, a consideration-generator whose output is to some degree undetermined produces a series of considerations, some of which may of course be immediately rejected as irrelevant by the agent (consciously or unconsciously). Those considerations that are selected by the agent as having more than a negligible bearing on the decision then figure in a reasoning process.[24]

He reconceives this 'random consideration-generator' later in his discussion as a 'random-*but-deterministic* generation process',[25] arguing that the assumption that a random neurological function ought to be causally undetermined is an unnecessary one.

Before tackling this hypothetical solution directly, it is worth noting that Dennett's general view of the human nervous system and its relationship to the actions which human beings engage in is silent on the question of how 'intentions' are realised in CNS activity. It is quite critical for Dennett that we think of the CNS as engaged in the 'implementation of [an] intention'[26] whenever we are acting. (In the lengthy discussion of the cognitivist approach to consciousness,[27] we read of human analogues to print-out components receiving '*orders to perform speech-acts*, or *semantic intentions*'.[28]) There is absolutely no argument adduced in defence of this way of speaking about 'intentions', and it causes a great deal of conceptual trouble when we attempt to relate Dennett's usage of the notion of intention to the logical grammar of 'intention'. If we are using the term 'intention' as it might ordinarily be used, it is abundantly clear that not every action we may properly be said to perform is the realisation of some prior intention to engage in it. *That* we have a prior intention now being implemented is something true about us only in certain circumstances of our acting (doing something). This mechanisation and universalisation of 'intending' as a prior neural event or prior something-or-other with a neural 'realisation' is a pure conceptual fiction.

Why is this important here? The link is to Dennett's (and others') propensity to mechanise vernacular concepts in the service of the illusory goal of a comprehensive neurophysiological/CNS account of human conduct in all of its aspects. In his discussion of the hypothetical 'random consideration-generator', he construes the concept of a consideration in a very idiosyncratic way, along with the correlative notions of 'accepting' or 'rejecting' a consideration. When I am properly claimed to be engaged in 'considering' something – an option for action, say – I am not thereby simply *inspecting* a series of 'considerations', let alone a series which *randomly* occurs. If I am introspecting randomly occurring images, sentences or some other 'internal' occurrences, then at best I may be described as daydreaming or letting my thoughts wander. To let one's thoughts wander is scarcely a proper procedure describable as 'considering' options prior to making a decision (and, of course, not *all* decisions, even important ones, presuppose a prior spate of reflection). If I am asked what I have 'taken into consideration' prior to arriving at a decision, it would be heard as immensely peculiar were I to state or describe some series of randomly occurring thoughts. The whole point about 'considering' and about 'considerations' is that they are things we do or take into account, and *not* things which *happen to* us or within us. Dennett's account eliminates everything that makes the crucial difference between considering, reasoning and arriving at a decision and merely being confronted with randomly occurring 'ideas' (some of which never make it through our endopsychic censor, our 'unconscious' relevance-checking procedures).

The central difficulty I have with Dennett's account is that it begs the essential questions which it was supposed to have (partially) resolved. The radical libertarian is not likely to be satisfied with a series of reformulations of intentional and/or agent-bound predicates into a collection of mechanistic process descriptions, even if he is prepared to admit that *some* mechanistic processes (whether deterministic or indeterministic) *do* occur in the brain so as to enable an agent to do those things to which purposes, intentions, volitions and so on are logically connected. It is because Dennett is so wedded *in principle* to the possibility (if not the practical possibility) of 'mapping deliberation processes onto neural activity'[29] that he settles for hypothetical solutions to the sentient-automata paradox which so utterly miss the point. The brain is consistently being described as engaged in activities which only persons can engage in, and there is no solution to the basic problem in shifting its focus in this way, even if it were remotely defensible conceptually.

6 SOME CONCLUDING REMARKS

The general *Weltanschauung* in the bio-behavioural sciences is likely to remain a mechanistic one, no matter how complicated become the forms in which mechanistic versions of CNS functioning are cast – whether they be cybernetic, indeterministic or other variants as yet obscure. This need not be any cause for epistemological concern unless the fundamental world-picture of nomological and probabilistic (or stochastic) processes is imported uncritically into our thinking about those orders of phenomena and their conceptualisation properly (i.e., logico-grammatically) bound up with the concept of *agency*. The irreducibility of agency to mechanism (in any of its forms) is a natural function of the different origins and purposes of these distinct conceptual domains. We have, for most of our history as a linguistic species, been involved in dealing with ourselves as organisms *simpliciter*. Our ways of reasoning about our ways of reasoning, our ways of thinking about the nature of thinking, etc., have developed (until relatively recently) in isolation from our theoretical interest in our own organic equipment, our nervous systems. We employ concepts, schemata and assumptions with a firm mechanistic stamp in treating natural phenomena in the current epoch – even quantum phenomena are thought by many to be amenable to some hitherto unknown form of reconciliation with that fundamental view of things. And yet, in the case of beings we think of as agents in the fullest sense, we face a peculiar tension quite unlike that confronted by theoretical physicists in rationalising the indeterminacies of quantum phenomena, a tension captured in the paradox of sentient-automata theorising.

The reason why the sentient-automata paradox appears so strikingly as an obstacle, standing in the way of our efforts to provide a naturalistic account of human agency consistent with biological and evolutionary fact and theory, is because we seek *a comprehensive and systematically unified world-picture*. It is because this yearning is so deep within us when we reflect upon our scientific versions of our world and of ourselves that we become impatient with our own conceptual systems, thinking them deficient to the extent that their logic of use appears to inhibit the unification we seek. We figure that such fundamental distinctions as the 'voluntary' and the 'involuntary', the 'willed' and the 'caused', the 'purposeful' and the 'random', may one day be brought together in the same system of explanatory principles, but continue to be frustrated even in our wildest philosophical Gedankenexperiments.

NOTES

1. Daniel C. Dennett, 'Mechanism and Responsibility' in his *Brainstorms: Philosophical Essays on Mind and Psychology* (Vermont: Bradford Books, 1978) p. 233.
2. Ibid., p. 246.
3. Ibid., p. 245 and *passim*.
4. Vivian M. Weil, 'Intentional and Mechanistic Explanation', *Philosophy and Phenomenological Research*, vol. XL, September 1979 – June 1980, p. 464.
5. John Thorp, *Free Will: A Defence Against Neurophysiological Determinism* (London: Routledge & Kegan Paul, 1980).
6. Ibid., p. 1.

7. Ibid., p. 16.
8. Ibid., pp. 67–71, and the discussion in ch. VI, 'The Random and the Free'.
9. Ibid., p. 71.
10. Roderick W. Chisholm, 'Responsibility and Avoidability' in Sidney Hook (ed.), *Determinism and Freedom in the Age of Modern Science* (New York: Collier Books, N.Y., 1961) p. 159.
11. Thorp, *Free Will*, p. 106.
12. Ibid., p. 107. Thorp is here grappling with the following issue, which is, I think, his central problem: 'Is there anything that the libertarian can say which, while telling us something more than just that agent causality is going on, would however not destroy his position by offering some events in the agent as what constitutes the agent causality?' (p. 107).
13. John Eccles, *The Neurophysiological Basis of Mind: Principles of Neurophysiology* (Oxford: Clarendon Press, 1953): Eccles, *The Understanding of the Brain* (London: McGraw-Hill, 1973) esp. p. 189, and Eccles and K. Popper, *The Self As Brain* (Oxford: Clarendon Press, 1979).
14. John Thorp, *Free Will*, p. 127.
15. Ibid.
16. Ibid.
17. Ludwig Wittgenstein, *Philosophical Investigations*, trans. G.E.M. Anscombe (Oxford: Basil Blackwell, 1968) paras 621–22. A.I. Melden, in a classic paper, 'Willing', in Alan R. White (ed.), *The Philosophy of Action* (Oxford: Oxford University Press, 1968) pp. 70–78, drew attention to the infinite-regress problem by claiming that for every act of a person there is an antecedent 'act of volition (of will)': for now we need to posit an antecedent act of volition for *this* act of volition, etc. Melden seems to settle for an unanalysable, primitive version of 'voluntarily moving a muscle' in which the *extra* notion of 'willing' is not invoked. However, he does not go into details about the (neuro-)physiological process involved and how *that* is to be conceptualised. Thorp's account at least has the value of raising this issue directly in connection with libertarian vs. mechanistic claims about the voluntary movement of one's muscles, the making of a free decision, and related problems.
18. Vivian M. Weil 'Explanation', p. 463. Weil is referring here to Norman Malcolm's paper, 'Explaining Behavior', *The Philosophical Review*, vol. 76, no. 2, January 1967.
19. Ludwig Wittgenstein, *Zettel*, trans. G.E.M. Anscombe: eds, G.E.M. Anscombe and G.H. von Wright (Oxford: Basil Blackwell, 1967) para. 46. See also para. 50: 'One may disturb someone in thinking – but in intending?'
20. J.F.M. Hunter, 'On How We Talk' in his *Essays After Wittgenstein* (Toronto: University of Toronto Press, 1973) p. 164.
21. This is a foundational assumption of Fodor's *The Language of Thought* (New York: Thomas Y. Crowell, 1975) along with much contemporary computational psychology.
22. David Wiggins, 'Towards a Reasonable Libertarianism' in Ted Honderich (ed.), *Essays on Freedom of Action* (London: Routledge &

Kegan Paul, 1973).
23. Daniel C. Dennett, 'On Giving Libertarians What They Say They Want' in *Brainstorms*.
24. Ibid., p. 295.
25. Ibid., p. 298, italics added.
26. Ibid., p. 291.
27. Dennett, 'Toward a Cognitive Theory of Consciousness' in *Brainstorms*.
28. Ibid., p. 156. Dennett elsewhere reifies 'intelligence', as in his remarks that 'the idea of intelligence exploiting randomness is not unfamiliar' (p. 293) and 'Intelligence makes the difference here because an intelligent selection and assessment procedure determines which microscopic indeterminacies get amplified.' (p. 295).
29. Ibid., p. 298.

6 On the intelligibility of experience

In what follows, I shall explore aspects of the relationship between language and intelligible experience.

1 OPAQUE ASCRIPTION CONTEXTS IN BEHAVIOURAL RESEARCH

How can we describe the experiences of non-linguistic or pre-linguistic creatures and remain 'true' to the ways in which they themselves actually experience things? The following problem characteristically arises when we attempt to do this, which I shall refer to as the *opacity/transparency elision*.[1] If I were to say of my pre-linguistic infant that he is watching the President on television, it is clear that I am describing the object of his watching from an *adult* point of view, which is one that he cannot literally be said to have. The 'adult' point of view is characterised as one involving experiences necessarily *conceptualised* for intelligibility and communication. If you say of me that I am sitting watching the President on television, it will imply that I know that it is the President whom I am watching; I have the concept of 'President'. Similarly, if you say of me that I am gazing at Sirius in the night sky, that can imply that I can pick out and name the star Sirius correctly; that I have the concept of 'Sirius'. However, with a pre-linguistic infant, when I say of him that he is busy watching the President on television (or something of this sort), I am conflating the way it is with the child with the way it is for me (and you) as a socialised concept-user. The opaque version of the child's perception may be rendered as 'watching Ø', where Ø can have a value only within the domain of concept-users (e.g., 'The President'). The transparent version of the child's perception (the one true for the observer) is simply that the child is watching the President on television, *only the implication of putting it this way is that it is also opaquely true (i.e., true for the child himself)*.

If one sought to be (excessively) precise, one might formulate a description of what the child was doing in the above instance as follows:

> The child is watching Ø such that *for us*, as concept-using experiencers, Ø is 'The President'.

The only cost of describing things this way is that it makes an ineffable mystery out of the Ø experienced by the child. There is no way to assign it a value without employing a concept alien to the child and thus inaccurate to his way of seeing, perceiving or experiencing. Even the great philosophical biologist von Uexküll,[2] who attempted to describe forms of 'animal consciousness' for sea urchins and other creatures, did not escape from this imputative difficulty. When he wrote, *inter alia*, that the world of the sea urchin is filled with 'sea urchin things',[3] he was clearly writing from the standpoint of the concept-using experiencer; so also was MacLeod when he wrote: 'A branch of a tree for Kohler's ape may be "something to swing from" and then "something with which to pull in a banana" '.[4] We are no closer this way to characterising how things are for pre-conceptual creatures than we are in assisting Nagel in his quest for 'What is it Like to be a Bat?'[5]

There is a very serious moral to be drawn from this opacity/transparency problem in characterising the world of the non-concept-using creature. Although we tolerate all sorts of anthropomorphic references in our ordinary parlance about our pets, etc. – indeed, it is difficult to say what the boundaries might be between a properly anthropomorphic imputation and an innocent extension of a concept-presupposing ascription – nonetheless, the unselfconscious usage of certain predicates in ascriptions to children without language is scientifically problematic.

An 'opaque ascription context' is one in which descriptions true of the same object(s) are not necessarily interchangeable *salva veritate*. If I judge that a man is six feet tall, I am not thereby judging him to be three and a half cubits in height. I may never have heard of a 'cubit' as a unit of measurement. Similarly, when we read that 'Oedipus wanted to marry Jocasta' we cannot interpret this, prior to the dreadful disclosure, to mean that Oedipus wanted to marry his mother, even though Jocasta was in fact Oedipus's mother. As Cooper notes: 'It is notoriously difficult, of course, to say just what descriptions are interchangeable in opaque contexts, and why. Certainly, though, the permissibility of substitution must have something to do with what a person would assent to or avow.'[6] Animals and pre-linguistic infants can neither assent to nor avow anything.

Let us consider some examples of how the problem of opaque ascription contexts arises in studies of experience. The first case which I would like to examine comes from a highly sensitive and interesting study by Goode of a congenitally deaf-blind girl identified for us as 'Chris'.[7] In the course of this study, Goode comes across the problem we are focusing upon here in the following terms. He is involved in trying to provide himself with 'an experiential basis for the kind of understanding' he sought by actively reproducing for himself the action-routines initiated by Chris. One of these involved her in manoeuvring him so that she was lying on his lap face up with his palm over her face and getting him to tap her right eyelid whilst she occasionally licked and sniffed his palm, humming 'seemingly melodic sounds'.[8] Goode remarks:

> I named this activity by the sound Chris produced while doing it, in order to remind myself, even in the reading of my own material, that my purpose was to burst the 'bubble'. To do this consistently I could not *properly* code my sensory experience of the activity into a natural language (as Chris apparently cannot do) because the 'bubble' and the 'language' were so intimately related that to sort one from the other would have been a

practical impossibility. Thus, in my first encounter with Chris's desired form of interactional activity, I became aware that in my writing about the activity I necessarily transformed what it was she could possibly intend in organising it as she did. The description I sought to suspend belief in was itself imbedded in the very language I used to formulate my attempt. I realized that *my enterprise was a standing contradiction.*[9]

Goode's frustration with having to take an 'external' point of view, in not being able to 'capture' Chris's experience and intentions in any other way except in terms of an apparatus unavailable to her, viz., a natural language, is symptomatic of investigators' troubles in doing phenomenological characterisations of experiences of non-concept-using persons. Not only are we unable to say what the activity amounted to for *Chris herself*, we are also unable to tell whether it actually amounted to *anything at all for her* unless we are prepared to assign 'pre-linguistic intentions' and then describe these 'intentions' in *conceptual* terms. It is here where we encounter the 'standing contradiction' of which Goode speaks.

The description, 'Chris experienced X', and the description, 'Chris had the intention to X in doing Y' involve opaque contexts in which the opacities cannot be resolved in the characteristic ways we have of resolving them for language-using experiencers. One result of this state of affairs in the case of Chris was that her conduct was accountable in 'multifaceted' ways. For Goode, she was in significant ways hedonistic and 'rational', whilst for the staff of the state hospital in which she was confined, she was 'faulted', singularly 'dumb'.[10] It is worth mentioning that the problem of handling an opaque ascription context analytically is enormously difficult even for those who recognise it in the course of their analysis: Goode at one point states: 'she focused on structuring the interaction so that she could get as much of what she inwardly recognised as 'good feelings', though I really don't "know" what these words index in terms of her experience.'[11] To say of Chris that she recognised something *as* 'good feelings' (inwardly?) is to predicate of her orientations a conceptualising capacity she manifestly lacked, hence Goode's subsequent rider to the effect that this could not genuinely be said of her. Although Chris was undoubtedly experiencing something, she could not *know* what it was, lacking the relevant concepts. The analytical ascription to such a person of experiential *knowledge*, of *conceptualised* experience, is an illegitimate but highly tempting move to make.

Hanna Pitkin, in her rich exposition of the philosophical work of the later Wittgenstein, touches upon this question as follows:

> It is tempting to say that the more an action approximates physical movements, can be done by animals or even objects, the less it hinges on intention, awareness, or concepts in [sic] the actor. Such actions do not require that the actor have a concept of the action. The more, conversely, an action is complex, abstract, governed by social conventions, compounded perhaps out of a variety of not entirely consistent language games, the less we can ascribe it to someone lacking the relevant concept, awareness, intention. Many activities of human beings can quite readily be ascribed to, performed by, children and animals . . . . Often things are complicated even with respect to a single verb; recall Wittgenstein's point that a dog can 'be afraid his master will beat him,' but not 'be afraid his master will beat him tomorrow'.[12]

There are numerous instances in the academic literature on child socialisation and language-acquisition in which caveats such as these are overlooked. We are told, e.g., that children *learn that* the cardinality of a set of objects is independent of its ordering (quite an abstract theorem) when the child has shown that the juxtapositions of the same number of objects does not confuse him in his preserving the same numerical count of them; that children discover *that* 'phenomic shape and intonation could co-vary independently';[13] that children 'possess' and 'comprehend' moral principles prior to their ability to express them[14] and that 'the child builds up the specific instances of the regulative principles of syntax as the necessary shape for his semantic intentions', which occurs as a result of the awareness that 'language use means the use of regulative principles.'[15] And, to take a blunder of my own, consider the following claim: 'the interlocutors analyse them (utterances) into *actions*'.[16] In all of these cases, an analytical version is being imputed to persons whose conduct and circumstances lack the necessary criteria for their *proper* imputation. Learning that, discovering that, becoming aware that, analysing as (or into): these are concept-requiring achievements and actions. Moreover, in the cited instances, the object complements are, on reflection, unavailable to those whose conduct formed the basis for their assignation. The over-intellectualisation of children (and others) is a function of failing to distinguish between opaque and transparent attribution contents – of eliding the opaque with the transparent version in a misleading way. I believe that it is quite a common problem in behavioural science accounts of the experiences and orientations of those who do not (fully) share the language and culture of those who are attempting to describe them.

An exactly opposite propensity is described by Wieder in a discussion of the research undertaken by some psychologists and ethnologists on chimpanzees in captivity.[17] Wieder remarks:

Perhaps nowhere is the incompatibility between behavioristic operationalism and the life-world more provocative than in the research arenas of the higher animal forms other than man. Here, the living organisms are at once persuasive about the fact of their own conscious lives when met face-to-face, and, at the same time, descriptions of those lives as conscious are subject to ridicule by other scientists. Researchers thus find themselves compelled to describe their chimpanzee or dolphin associates as without consciousness and to contrive experiments that are reportable without referring to animals as subjects, while living along with those same animals as fellow subjects and, paradoxically, counting on this subject-to-subject relationship with them to conduct experiments that are reportable in behavioristic-operationalist terms.[18]

Wieder quotes from an account of Temerlin's, derived from the latter's famous monograph: *Lucy – Growing Up Human*. Temerlin's general policy is depicted by Wieder as one of 'not describing Lucy's phenomenal world'.[19] However, as Wieder notes, where Temerlin described Lucy (a chimp) as engaged in such activities as 'turning off the machine [a vacuum cleaner]', 'picking up her unfinished glass of gin', 'contemplating the pictures in the *National Geographic*', 'leafing through the magazine' and 'masturbating', in such passages he did not – could not? – eliminate the cultural concepts in terms of which the chimpanzee's conduct and its object-environment is intelligibly communicated to acculturated readers of the research report. Wieder goes on to argue that chimpanzee researchers simply *must* employ the cultural resources we have for describing, orienting to, manipulating and motivating their chimps, but that much of this reliance upon the linguistically constituted conceptual apparatus disappears from their subsequent research reports due to a fear of 'anthropomorphism' and a methodologically ordained adherence to 'physicalistic' depictions. As a result of this methodological 'purge', such reports do not convey *enough* relevant information, or mislead their readers in significant respects.

Here, then, we have a contrasting case to the one encountered above in which the temptation was to attribute (by implication or by explicit design) conceptual resources to subjects lacking them; in the cases discussed by Wieder, the temptation is to rid oneself even of those intention-dependent and culture-dependent characterisations which are an integral part of construing an organism *as a subject who acts* (rather than an automaton with neither plans nor purposes). Since it is manifest at once to an observer who freely employs the 'life-world' modes of conceptualisation that, e.g., chimpanzees *are* conscious subjects, then to the extent that an alternative mode of conceptualisation is employed to constitute the *explananda* (e.g., operationalistic behaviourism of the Duncan and Fiske variety[20]), distortions and misrepresentations can always be found by those who maintain the primacy of the 'natural standpoint' of the lifeworld (our mundane conceptual schemata).

2 THE CONCEPTUAL PHENOMENOLOGY OF EXPERIENCE

If we characterise 'basic experiences' as facilitated by the senses, as we must (e.g., vision, hearing, taste, touch and the olfactory), then of course any creature with a nervous system and one or more of these sensory modalities can be credited with having experiences. The problems arise when, for other than *practical* purposes, we seek to characterise *the content of sensory information* for concept-less creatures. As Dretske notes,

> We either do not know what the semantic content of their internal state is or we suspect that, if they have a content, it may not be expressible in *our* language.[21]

Take a vernacular specification such as: 'Our dog recognised the postman this morning and wagged at him as usual.' What constrains us against complete acceptance of this as a wholly accurate and adequate characterisation of what the dog experienced is the realisation that the concept of 'postman' carries *for us* an array of conceptual implications and relations (a great deal more semantic content) than it could possibly carry for the animal. And our qualms are not fully satisfied by 'reducing' the category to putatively more 'primitive' components, such as 'intruder', 'man', 'animate being' and the like. Each of these concepts (contrary to Dretske) function in very complex ways in various language-games and cannot be analysed as 'ostensively learned simple concept(s)'[22] at all. We are, in fact, not really saying of a dog that it *understands the concept* of a 'man' or of an 'intruder' when we predicate of it the recognition of a man or an intruder, let alone that it has *beliefs* about them (again, *contra* Dretske). We are locating in its behaviour and the circumstances sufficient grounds for extending by analogy the semantics of our own experiential life to the animal.

Animals without concepts (without symbolic media for expression in criterially-grounded ways) are, of course, receiving sensory information about the world which we can often correctly characterise using our language. Experimental and ethnological evidence can inform us of animals' capacities for experiential discriminations of simple objects, colours, patterns, and a large array of phenomena which we are tempted to refer to as 'brute' or 'raw' sensory input. In our practical dealings with animals, especially those domesticated for our use and/or enjoyment, we have occasion to incorporate them more fully into our ways of talking about the world than we would have as purely detached observers of their natural conduct and dispositions. And yet, for a variety of cases there are simply no decidability algorithms such as exist for (on occasion) telling what a language-user is experiencing. And there exist a host of cases in which we simply rule out particular experiences as beyond the animals' capacities; most if not all of these are experiences which logically presuppose linguistic capacities.

It remains, however, very difficult to say in *general* terms when we are right and when we are flatly wrong to make experiential predications to non- or pre-linguistic organisms. For a variety of experiential predications are in a strong sense *underdetermined* by purely non-linguistic forms of behaviour and their surrounding circumstances. That we may elect to make a determination for some purpose, and be justified in doing so for that purpose, does not gainsay the point that we may not be able to reject some alternative determination out of hand. Many animals are, for us, at once both familiar and alien, both transparent and inscrutable. The success of evolutionary theory encourages us to believe that we do indeed share more than we fail to share in experiential terms with the higher primates. And yet, our own pre-linguistic infants pose for us similar questions about the form of the world they dwell within. There are no incorrigible criteria for telling how they *perceptually* represent their physical environments. Whether whatever they do see, hear, smell etc. carries *accurate information* about the environments within which they live is detectable from what they do and are disposed to do within those environments, but this in itself gives no incorrigible support for any given version of what they actually see, hear, smell and so forth. In a striking passage, Dretske makes the following comment:

Practical success in responding to someone's presence on my front porch, even when this success is to be explained in auditory terms, does not imply that I can hear people on my front porch. And, for the same reason, the rabbit's success in evading the fox should not be taken to imply that the rabbit can see, hear, or smell the fox. It *may*, of course, but it will take more than facts about the rabbit's cognitive abilities to establish this conclusion.[23]

The underdetermination of actual experience (on occasion) by reference to conduct and circumstances is not meant to be a phenomenological equivalent to Quine's thesis about the 'inscrutability of reference'.[24] After all, for 'reference' (and 'experience') to mean anything at all, there have to be instances fully described in which doubts have no legitimate place. What is being noted here is simply this: given the occurrence of some situations in which accurate information is being conveyed and acted upon by an organism, no given experiential attribution may be entailed; indeed, more than one experiential attribution can 'fit the facts' with equivalent adequacy. And such situations often arise with animal and pre linguistic infant attributions. The linguistic institution of 'telling' someone what was seen, heard, touched, smelt or tasted is indeed critical in enabling us to disambiguate many cases for concept-using experiencers, but even here there can be no absolute subjective sovereignty. We can accuse persons of hallucinations, of delusions, of mistaken beliefs, of being the victims of illusions, etc., when their claims lack intersubjective warrantability.

Because we cannot recollect (as distinct from being under the impression that we can recollect) what our experiences of the world were like before we acquired any language, we are tempted to follow William James's characterisation of the neonate's world as one of 'booming, buzzing confusion'. This too is a mythical construction. What attribution criteria could it have? And could they really be satisfied in all cases for all (normal) infants? One would expect at least that all children would continue to be terribly disoriented, clasping their hands to their ears, until the first inklings of language could be imparted to them. What was James driving at here?

I think that such descriptions are motivated by considerations such as the following. Acquiring language entails acquiring means for (*inter alia*) making sense of the experienced world (including the states of one's own 'inner world' as well). When we reflect upon the notion of an environment (or even a single object) as being *totally devoid of sense*, we are at a loss to grasp how that could be experienced. Our concepts and our experienced world are not in a relation of lamination, but of *imbrication*. Yet we know, rationally, that non-linguistic beings with developed nervous systems, etc., do indeed inhabit a world that is utterly senseless, totally devoid of meaning. This is *not* to say that their world is utterly devoid of *information*, an insight well exploited by Dretske to whom I owe this important distinction.[25] But Dretske's difficulties in giving non-question-begging characterisations of the semantics of this information testify to the point being advanced here: once acculturated, there is simply no looking back, no concept-free ways of 'getting at' the 'realities'. Kant's difficulties with the 'noumenal realm' and Kuhn's problem in giving 'neutral' characterisations of phenomena subjected to diverse forms of conceptualisation in different scientific paradigms[26] attest to the timelessness of this constraint. As Feyerabend has remarked, phenomena and their ways of being described are typically encountered by members as 'firmly glued together'; he notes:

> This unity is the result of a process of learning that starts in one's childhood. From our very early days we learn to react to situations with the appropriate responses, linguistic or otherwise. The teaching procedures both *shape* the 'appearance' or 'phenomenon', and establish a firm *connection* with words, so that finally the phenomena seem to speak for themselves without outside help or extraneous knowledge. They *are* what the associated statements assert them to be. The language

they 'speak' is, of course, influenced by the beliefs of earlier generations which have been held for so long that they no longer appear as separate principles, but enter the terms of everyday discourse, and, after the prescribed training, seem to emerge from the things themselves.[27]

Considerations such as these contribute, I believe, to the argument which would assert *the primacy of conceptualisation over experience or consciousness* in phenomenology, and which would prompt us to revise our phenomenological programme accordingly. 'Structures' of consciousness can only be structures of conceptualisation, and it is precisely this which renders much of our phenomenological appreciation of pre-conceptual creatures analogical rather than literal. J.L. Austin, a major representative of the school of 'linguistic philosophy', a school taken to be wholly opposed to the traditions of phenomenology, had this to say:

> In view of the prevalence of the slogan 'ordinary language', and of such names as 'linguistic' or 'analytic' philosophy or 'the analysis of language', one thing needs specially emphasising to counter misunderstandings. When we examine what we should say when, what words we should use in what situations, we are looking again not *merely* at words (or 'meanings', whatever they may be) but also at the realities we use the words to talk about: we are using a sharpened awareness of words to sharpen our perception of, though not as the final arbiter of, the phenomena. For this reason, I think it might be better to use, for this way of doing philosophy, some less misleading name than those given above – for instance, 'linguistic phenomenology', only that is rather a mouthful.[28]

It is perhaps also instructive in this connection to find Wittgenstein remarking in a conversation with Drury: 'You could say of my work that it is "phenomenology"' ',[29] although there are many significant points of contrast between Wittgenstein's later writings (which he was working on at the time of this remark) and the work of Husserl, Heidegger and others in the phenomenological movement.

3 TOWARD A RECONSTRUCTION OF SCHUTZ'S CONSTITUTIVE PHENOMENOLOGY OF THE NATURAL ATTITUDE

Alfred Schutz's celebrated project, *The Phenomenology of the Social World*, remains a source of critical inspiration for all students of the nature of relationships between individual persons and the social realities which they create and sustain.[30] However, many commentators (including myself on prior occasions) have expressed reservations about some of Schutz's central concepts and their adequacy for advancing his project.[31] In this concluding section, therefore, I want to attempt a sympathetic sketch, in the light of the foregoing discussion, of some of the ways in which a closer attention to the logical grammar of communication and conceptualisation can overcome these theoretical obstacles.

First, consider Schutz's general argument about the foundation of 'meaning' in the life-world. He takes it that the meanings which objects, events, situations and persons have for us in everyday life are endowed to them by *acts* of consciousness, in Husserlian terms. He speaks of the 'meaning-endowing' experiences of consciousness, and argues that 'only the already experienced is meaningful, not that which is being experienced'.[32] Only in a retrospective glance are segments of the otherwise 'undifferentiated' flow of experiences rendered intelligible to us.[33]

How is this to be rendered so as to preserve the insights embedded in it whilst at the same time reconciling it with the actual data of praxis and experience as they are lived in the real world? For it is surely not an acceptable characterisation of our experience to claim for it that it is only differentiated by acts of retrospective assessment or 'interpretation'. I am not aware of inhabiting an ongoingly meaningless stream of experiences which I must constantly interrupt in order to attribute or endow them with meanings. It is, indeed, impossible properly to imagine a world in which 'only the already experienced is meaningful' whilst the ongoing present involvement(s) of a subject lack any intelligibility. Of course, retrospective assessments can lead us to see more clearly, or differently, what was going on around us or to us, but it seems to be a fundamental datum of human existence *consequent upon the acquisition of a conceptual apparatus* that we experience not some putative 'raw sensory data' but familiar scenes or unfamiliar but intelligible ones for the most part as we live our lives. The pre-givenness of the intelligibility of our environments is theoretically inaccessible to us if we follow Schutz's formulations strictly. Moreover, various forms of 'differentiation' are available in our ongoing experiences of many kinds, as we pass (pre-reflectively, indeed, for the most part) through the myriad phases and sequences of activity. I think that Schutz has extrapolated far too broadly here from the particular cases in which we confront situations which are experienced as inherently ambiguous or confusing and must situatedly reflect upon them, employing our conceptual schemata to do so. From here, I would argue that we must avoid equating meaning *per se* with 'a certain way of directing one's gaze at an item of one's own experiences',[34] for such an equation would rule out a distinction which is vital to that *Lebenswelt* which Schutz is seeking to elucidate, viz., a distinction between correctly (or properly, or adequately) discerning the meaning of 'an item of one's own experience' and *in*correctly doing so. Meaning cannot be, as Wittgenstein and Austin have helped us to acknowledge, a 'mental' act or process nor anything which an individual can have sovereignty in establishing (even though individuals can have such a sovereignty when 'meaning' is construed as 'special significance', and not in terms of the basic intelligibility structures of phenomena).

One of Husserl's most important insights was essentially a *conceptual* (logico-grammatical) one, in my view. It consisted in showing that the concepts of 'consciousness' and 'experience' could not stand alone, but were necessarily tied, even if tacitly, to object-complements. There is no 'consciousness' *per se*, but only consciousness *of* (. . .). Husserl, however, tended to treat the grammatical property of intentionality as an active property of consciousness itself, thence proposing that our experiences 'endow meaning', and that our consciousness 'comprises many intentional Acts'. In this way, an elementary insight becomes

obfuscated since we now wonder how 'experience' or 'consciousness' could possibly engage in 'acts' of any kind. Persons with
consciousness can act, but how can consciousness itself act? Such
a claim negates the very point about which Husserl had made his
strongest argument, namely that there can only be consciousness
(experience) *of*, never 'consciousness-in-itself'.

Following Husserl, Schutz writes of 'Acts of both external and
internal experience', claiming that as one looks back on elapsed
experience, it can be seen in a unitary, discrete ('monothetic')
way 'even though it has come into existence in phases and
through many intentional Acts'.[35] In one sense, of course, it is
clear that various kinds of experiences which I have undergone
were features of courses of activity which I *as a person* was engaged
in, such as noticing something, paying particular attention to
some things and not to others, recalling similar past situations,
being momentarily distracted as I turned to related considerations, and the like. However, it is not at this level that Schutz's
account is operative: he is, following Husserl, proposing that, for
any external object, 'the object is constituted out of appearances
as we encounter them in our stream of consciousness'.[36]
Although this is often true, as when we detect something unclear
in our perceptual field and then 'get a clearer perspective' on it,
thus seeing what it really is and not just what it initially appeared
to have been, such a description cannot capture the *general form* of
our relationship to objects in the world. And, throughout Schutz's
entire discussion of 'The Constitution of Meaningful Lived
Experience',[37] there is scarcely a mention of the role of
language, of a conceptual apparatus. Schutz's procedure is clearly
to start from a 'solitary Ego'[38] and work *outwards* to intersubjective language and culture, and it is this inadequate starting-point
which causes him so much trouble in specifying the relationship(s)
between the individual as a social, acculturated being and the
sociocultural resources which enable him to exist as such.

Nonetheless, if such difficulties are cleared away, we find in
Schutz's work a valuable stress upon the centrality of 'constitution' as a core problem for theoretical elucidation in cognitive
analysis. Instead of seeing it as an omnipresent problem,

however, I think that it is more fruitfully approached as a *members'* problem which arises, is solved or not solved, in distinctive ways in the real, social lives they lead. In other words, the 'constitution' of phenomena – which is largely a matter of the *conceptualisation* of phenomena for certain purposes – is investigable as a routine practical problem in various (organisational and other) contexts in which people must assemble decisions, categorise events, objects and persons, and where they exhibit reasoning procedures and investigative methods appropriate to their courses of practical activity. This view naturally leads us into the domain of ethnomethodological studies, and when implemented as a research directive shows clearly the relevance of linking the phenomenological concern to the study of the (informal) logic of linguistic conceptualisation.

A major corrective, then, to the Schutzian programme is to insist upon the relevance of what Wittgenstein termed 'criteria' for practical conceptualisation in everyday life. Criteria are defeasible, conventional evidences for the constitution of phenomena, and they are inextricably linked to the differential distribution of practical interests in social existence. The constitution (conceptualisation) of a dead body as either (i) a corpse, (ii) a cadaver,[39] (iii) a suicide, (iv) an accident-victim, (v) a case of euthanasia, (vi) a homicide, (vii) a 'naturally' dead person or (viii) an undecidable case, will depend upon the domains of practical interest in it (by incumbents of different social categories, e.g., spouse, police officer, coroner, mortician, G.P., jurors, etc.) and upon the invocation of domain-sensitive 'criteria'.[40] And in *some* instances, the very characterisation of a body *as* indeed a dead one will be problematic, requiring the invocation, use, argument over and decision about criteria for *those* relevances. There is no possibility of sustaining the claim that 'the constitution of meaningful lived experience' can be elucidated independently of its contexts of differential relevance and purpose as a unitary phenomenon, or even as an omnipresent phenomenon. Yet neither should there be any doubt about the importance of elucidating constitutive *practices* as they occur in social life.

NOTES

1. The terms 'opacity' and 'transparency' are taken from W. V. Quine's *Word and Object* (Cambridge, Mass.: M.I.T. Press, 1960). The 'elision' in question arises when an opaque version of something (i.e., a version true for the perceiver) is conflated with a transparent version (i.e., a version true for the observer of the perceiver).

2. Baron J.J. von Uexküll, *Umwelt und Innenwelt der Tiere* (Berlin: Springer, 1909); cited in J.S. Lansing, 'In the World of the Sea Urchin' in A.L. Becker and A.L. Yengoyan (eds), *The Imagination of Reality* (New York: Ablex, 1979) esp. pp. 77–9.

3. Ibid., p. 77.

4. R.B. MacLeod, 'Phenomenology: A Challenge to Experimental Psychology' in T.W. Wann (ed.), *Behaviorism and Phenomenology: Contrasting Bases for Modern Psychology* (Phoenix: University of Chicago, 1967) p. 68. When MacLeod asserts: 'quite dogmatically, that no experience is devoid of meaning', (ibid.) it is unclear whether he has in mind the opaque or transparent availability of the experience. For a human observer, these ways of characterising the ape's experiences may well be cogent and subserve practical strategies; they tell us nothing about their 'meaning' for the animal, and I think the whole notion of 'meaningful experience' (as contrasted with, say, informational content in a strict sense – see below) remains radically unclear in this context.

5. Thomas Nagel, 'What is it Like to be a Bat?' as reprinted in Ned Block (ed.), *Readings in Philosophy of Psychology*, vol. *1* (Cambridge, Mass.: Harvard University Press, 1980).

6. David E. Cooper, *Knowledge of Language* (New York: Humanities Press, 1975) p. 90.

7. David Goode, 'The World of the Congenitally Deaf-Blind: Toward the Grounds for Achieving Human Understanding' in Howard Schwartz and Jerry Jacobs (eds), *Qualitative Sociology: A Method to the Madness* (New York: Free Press, 1979).

8. Ibid., p. 388.

9. Ibid.

10. Ibid., p. 392.

11. Ibid.

12. Hanna F. Pitkin, *Wittgenstein and Justice: On the Significance of Ludwig Wittgenstein for Social and Political Thought* (Los Angeles, Calif.: University of California Press, 1972) p. 255.

13. Jenny Cook-Gumperz, 'The Child as Practical Reasoner' in M. Sanches and B. Blount (eds), *Sociocultural Dimensions of Language Use* (New York: Academic Press, 1975) p. 144.

14. For some discussion of these Piagetian claims, see L. Kohlberg, 'Stage and Sequence: The Cognitive Development Approach to Socialization' in D. Goslin (ed.), *Handbook of Theory and Research in Socialization* (Chicago: Rand-McNally, 1969).

15. Cook-Gumperz, 'Child as Reasoner', p. 143. (None of this detracts in the least, however, from the many good arguments in this article.)

16. J. Coulter, *The Social Construction of Mind* (London: Macmillan, 1979) p. 27. Taken literally, this would construe ordinary speaker-hearers as conversation-analysts coming up with illocutionary characterisations on an utterance-by-utterance basis, something they manifestly do not engage in. Here I fell into the very trap of over-intellectualising mundane achievements against which I had been arguing in many places in the book. (I could add that this testifies to the pervasiveness of the practice; no critic of my book spotted the mistake, which is, by now, a fairly standard one to make in programmatic and philosophical discussions of ethnomethodology and conversation analysis. It might be harmless except that it is often a tacit basis for erecting neo-cognitivist versions of those enterprises).

17. D. Lawrence Wieder, 'Behavioristic Operationalism and the Life-World: Chimpanzees and Chimpanzee Researchers in Face-to-Face Interaction', *Sociological Inquiry*, vol. 50, nos 3–4, 1980. (Special Issue on Language and Social Interaction, edited by Don Zimmerman and Candace West).

18. Ibid., p. 77.

19. Ibid., p. 84.

20. S. Duncan and D. Fiske, *Face-to-Face Interaction: Research, Methods and Theory* (New Jersey: Erlbaum, 1977).

21. Fred I. Dretske, *Knowledge and the Flow of Information* (Cambridge, Mass.: M.I.T. Press, 1981) p. 209.

22. Ibid., p. 212. It was Wittgenstein who demonstrated that ostensive training alone cannot suffice for inculcating conceptual knowledge in a child. For an excellent discussion of 'ostensive training' and language acquisition, see Bernard Harrison, *Meaning and Structure: An Essay in the Philosophy of Language* (New York: Harper & Row, 1972) pp. 49–02.

23. Dretske, *Knowledge*, p. 168. Also: 'The fact that I answer the door every time someone depresses the door button, the fact that I am so extraordinarily sensitive to the position of the door button, does not mean that I can *hear* (or somehow *sense*) the button being depressed.' (Ibid., p. 167).

24. W.V. Quine, 'The Inscrutability of Reference' (excerpted from his Dewey Lectures delivered at Columbia University, 1968) in Danny D. Steinberg and Leon A. Jakobovits (eds), *Semantics* (Cambridge: Cambridge University Press, 1971).

25. Dretske, Cambridge: *Knowledge*.

26. Thomas S. Kuhn, *The Structure of Scientific Revolutions* International Encyclopoedia of Unified Science (Chicago: University of Chicago Press, 1970). For an excellent assessment of Kuhn's attempt to locate a 'neutral' position from which to characterise phenomena differentially conceived of in different scientific traditions, see Pitkin *Wittgenstein and Justice*, pp. 111–15. For a Wittgensteinian appraisal of Kuhn's views, see Derek L. Phillips, *Wittgenstein and Scientific Knowledge* (London: Macmillan, 1977).

27. Paul Feyerabend, *Against Method* (New York: Verso/Schocken Books, 1980) p. 72. Feyerabend, despite a distinguished reputation as a

Wittgenstein exegesist, has little that is positive to say of what he calls 'linguistic analysis' in this text. He maintains that everyday language embodies past beliefs and theoretical sediments which ought to be disentangled in order that we might achieve a clearer perspective upon our commitments in judging what there is in the world. However, he does not seem to me to have made a case for construing all of everyday conceptualisation in this way, and in the quotation in my text I think his use of the word 'statements', rather than 'concepts', betrays an excessively discursive and constative view of linguistic functioning. Statements (such as: 'the moon follows me as I walk') might appear innocuous and literally descriptive but might indeed be falsely taken to be 'pure observational statements' which constrain us against grasping the non-obvious facts about the relative motion of earth and moon. *Concepts*, however, require an altogether different treatment, and even Feyerabend cannot avoid relying upon their conventional meanings to make his own case. Ordinary language indeed contains misleading 'truisms' which ought occasionally to be unpacked, but it contains as well many (if not all) of the concepts with which any such unpacking might be accomplished.

28. J.L. Austin, *Philosophical Papers*, eds J.O. Urmson and G.J. Warnock (Oxford: Oxford University Press, 1970), p. 182. The quotation comes from Austin's famous paper, 'A Plea for Excuses'.

29. M. O'C. Drury, 'Conversations with Wittgenstein' in Rush Rhees (ed.), *Ludwig Wittgenstein: Personal Recollections* (New Jersey: Rowman & Littlefield, 1981), p. 131.

30. Alfred Schutz, *The Phenomenology of the Social World*, trans. George Walsh and Frederick Lehnert (USA: Northwestern University Press, 1967).

31. For a useful, recent discussion, see Richard J. Bernstein, *The Restructuring of Social and Political Theory* (Philadelphia: University of Pennsylvania Press, 1978), Part iii: 'The Phenomenological Alternative'.

32. Ibid., p. 52.

33. Ibid., p. 51.

34. Ibid., p. 42. (Schutz places this claim in italics in his text).

35. Ibid., p. 76.

36. Ibid., pp. 78–9.

37. This is the title of Part 11 of *The Phenomenology of the Social World*.

38. Ibid., p. 96.

39. For a witty discussion of the problem of words-and-world elucidated by the dead-body/corpse/cadaver distinctions in connection with the claim that they are different names for 'the same thing', see Pitkin, *Wittgenstein and Justice*, pp. 99–100.

40. A superb short research report in which the negotiable constitution of deaths as suicides is analysed is J.M. Atkinson's 'Societal Reactions to Suicide: The Role of Coroners' Definitions' in Stan Cohen (ed.), *Images of Deviance* (London: Penguin, 1972).

7 On defining cognition sociologically

Mental predicates, in all their variety, belong firmly within the social matrix of concept formation and usage. In earlier work, I was concerned to exploit this fact in the service of undermining the twin doctrines of mentalism and behaviourism;[1] mental predicates are not properly analysed as either names for putatively private, inner phenomena nor as names for constellations of behavioural events. Of course, this in no way contradicts the mundane experiences of silent soliloquies, mental images or dreams ('inner' events) nor the critical relevance of observable conduct for understanding the meanings and functions of mental concepts. However, the view that 'mind' is either a private repository of the things or events putatively labelled by our mental vocabulary ('mentalism') and the twin view (developed as its antithesis) that 'mind' is a (fictional) construction out of behavioural events *per se* (or dispositions to behave *per se*) – behaviourism (especially of the 'methodological' or 'logical' variety) – are *together* misleading and at best partial approximations to the appreciation of the nature of the mental and its proper conceptualisation.

My aim here is not to repeat the arguments employed to buttress this general claim (many of which derived from the Wittgensteinian analysis of the logical grammar of mental predicates). I want instead to focus upon further ramifications of what I have called a 'social constructionist' approach to the mental. 'Social constructionism', as I understand it in the present context, is not the assertion of *any* unitary doctrine or 'theory' about the mind at all, but rather proposes a study policy with the following basic principle: *treat the 'mental' properties of persons as generated from situated, constitutive practices*. Such practices include the manifold ways in which members avow, ascribe, deny, ratify, infer, argue about and in other ways deal with the appropriateness, intelligibility or warrantability of the range of 'mental' phenomena. In other words, whatever 'mental' (subjective, affective, experiential, cognitive) features persons are accredited with are to be investigated as embedded within courses of practical affairs. All judgments, inferences and attributions concerning the 'mental' are investigable for their conventionalities and constraints within a praxiological frame of reference.

In this way, I would argue, a sociologist of cognition (as distinct from a classical sociologist of knowledge) is in a position to locate the distinctive modes characterising, say, 'remembering' in courtroom settings (and the attendant criteria for warrantability and defeasibility, etc.); 'having a motive' in a psychiatric examination or a pre-trial hearing; having a kind of sensation in a dentist's surgery, and so on. There is nothing in this programme requiring the sociologist to become an eliminative materialist in respect of, say, 'occurrent mental events' such as conjuring up a mental image, having a sudden thought strike one, engaging in a silent soliloquy or dreaming about something. *Any* one-sided and reductionist view of such phenomena (quite independent of the many serious logical obstacles to its justification) would be utterly self-defeating and stipulative. After all, such occurrent mental states or events are routinely made topical within communicative interaction sequences, become assignable between persons in the context of their activities and in many other ways enter into intersubjective relations.

In what follows, I shall provide some study sketches to illustrate aspects of the collaborative production and management of accounts of 'subjective phenomena', elaborating upon various theoretical implications which they seem to me to have for the more general characterisation of the nature of human cognition and experience.

1 CONVENTIONAL EQUIVOCALITIES IN THE RATIFICATION OF SUICIDE-INTENTION AVOWALS

Social workers, especially those charged with handling referrals of a possibly psychiatric nature from members of the community, confront as a routine feature of their work the following problem. On occasion, someone will announce in their presence an intention to commit suicide. Strictly speaking I should write 'intention', because an equivocality conventionally attends locutions produced by community members such as: 'I'm going to kill myself'. For example, in one of the very few instances which I have recorded from my own researches, this announcement was embedded in the following sequence:

A: so I'm gonna *kill* myself
   (2.0)
B: You don't really *me::an* that. Let's talk about these problems some more.

An (apparent) intention-avowal concerning self-destruction was countered by the psychiatric aide in the immediately subsequent turn with an expression of disbelief, amounting to not acknowledging the avowal of a suicidal intention on the part of the interlocutor. Although more conversation did persuade the psychiatric aide of the seriousness, of the *reality*, of the intention-avowal, a first preference for their dealings with first occurrences of suicide intention-avowals is to withhold ratification.

What accounts for this conventional orientation? For the domain of practice we call 'psychiatric social work', and possibly for other, cognate domains, first-person disclosures of suicidal intention are subject to scrutiny for other functions they might be heard to be serving apart from, or in contrast to, their apparent function of merely declaring an intention. In other words, their own possibly motivated character is inspected in the light of biographical and contextual contingencies. A suicide-intention avowal might thereby turn out to have been, for practical purposes of subjectivity-determination, informed by some *ulterior* motive or purpose. Among these, a favoured option is that of 'attention-seeking'. Consider these remarks recorded during a conversation between two professional psychiatric social workers:

> Errm, I *do* find if a person talks to me about suicide in a threatening manner it doesn't bother me, it doesn't over-concern me when I go away. It's the people who *don't* talk about it, the people who hide it – one boy, I interviewed him and as far as I was aware the interview went reasonably well, he had a long history of mental illness, very fixed delusions that he was very grotesque, but these, this interview was no different from many others we'd had err . . . and two hours later he gassed himself. Err, these are the ones that *I* feel, errm, very guilty about.
> – Yeah.
> – *Very* guilty. These are the ones that make me feel inadequate, rather than the ones who want you to pay their rates bill or they want you to get them a change of council house and threaten to put their head in the gas-oven if you don't. The only problem with this type of person is that, with this sort of attention-seeking, manipulating manner, there's always the chance that they have the accident. But, errm, this doesn't bother me I can view it in this light and not feel terribly guilty about it.

Several themes emerge from this (and many similar) conversations on the topic of suicide-intention declarations held between professional mental health operators. A primary one concerns the conventional presupposition that *genuinely* suicidal persons may not be the ones to articulate any such intention prior to acting. Suicidalness, or at least its genuine presence in a given case, becomes a property more readily discernible without its explicit avowal, although maintaining this view is naturally somewhat risky. Talking someone out of his suicidalness can often begin with denying the expressed intention, but making an inference about the presence of suicidalness and taking action on its basis – something done several times during my researches into the work of psychiatric social workers – in the *absence* of any first-person avowal, carries its own attendant risks in the form of being called upon to justify the action in the face of someone's persistent *disavowals* of the intention.[2]

Treating certain cases of suicide-intention avowals as instances of 'attention-seeking' can be consequential for the subsequent characterisation of the mode of death. If enough relevant personnel in the community have been convinced of the initially 'manipulative' character of the intention-avowal, a subsequent death which might otherwise have been attributed to suicide may now be thought of as an 'accident' suffered during the course of a dramaturgical performance designed to advance the purposes for which the originally 'manipulative' declaration of intention was itself made. In this way, moreover, the possibility of guilt on the part of the recipient of the original avowal may be lessened or, in Henslin's terms, 'neutralised.'[3]

Another psychiatric social worker made the following observations:

> we don't automatically take somebody into hospital . . . because they say they intend to commit suicide. . . . We have to make – try and make – a judgment as to whether it's an attention-seeking err episode, or not. Errm, sometimes we're wrong and the patient is taken into hospital. Errm, whether this does him any harm . . . is errm, a matter of some doubt. It might, err . . . if this really, if he really wasn't intending suicide err, but errm, didn't bargain for getting admission to hospital.

In some measure, the transformability of an initially insincere intention-avowal into a state of genuine suicidalness may be contingent upon the course of action taken with respect to it by mental health authorities. This theme occurred several times in discussions with psychiatric personnel. Finally, we have in the following extract a quite direct reference to the view that first-person suicide-intention declarations are investigable by recipients for some ulterior motive:

> I think what it does is . . . is make you errm . . . look for what's

making him *say* this . . . you know, does he really mean it or, more often than not, what is he expecting from *you*? You know, from saying that 'I'm going to commit suicide', quite often I've found that it's errm . . . a way of pressurising you over into doing . . . err, taking some, some action. Errm, . . . it's usually quite subtle though . . . . But I don't think there are very many genuine suicide risks . . . I – I think the – you know – sombody who actually comes and, and says it . . . to you, like that. I . . . wouldn't worry too much.

It is in this area of intention-avowals where one can find most perspicuously the truth in the claim that they are not incorrigible, first-person reports of mental states or processes but *defeasible* commitment-claims about actions not to be expected in the normal course of events. Moreover, it is in this domain also where one can find a particularly close tie between intention-avowals and assignable *motives*, motives which may have little to do with the action being projected as the one actually intended. At every point, any such intention-avowal may be subject to scrutiny in the light of contextual relevances some of which may be out of the control of, or even the knowledge of, the one who declares the intention.

2 THE PRODUCTION AND TREATMENT OF 'FORGETTING' IN COURT HEARINGS

In a stimulating paper, Steinar Kvale argued that 'how an event is remembered depends upon the context in which it is perceived, retained *and* retrieved.'[4] By extension, how an event may be claimed as forgotten is also a function of the context of its relevance.

In a recent doctoral dissertation, Neustein has shown clearly that court hearings are domains of discourse within which recollections and failures to recollect take on a local and specific import for interlocutors.[5] I want to present here an extract, collected by Neustein, in which the cross-examining attorney is

questioning a police officer. The standing charge is that one of the
police officers involved in a case may have removed incriminating
evidence.

1. ATTORNEY: There were no o:ther bullets (0.1) that
you know of?
2. WITNESS: *Not* that I know of.
3. ATTORNEY: Detective I ---, did any other officers
search this car? or were in the car before
you got into it?
4. WITNESS: I: can:'t recall – There were other
officers at the car but I can't recall if any
officers went hh in:*to* the automobile.
5. ATTORNEY: So you don't *know* if one of the officers
move:d the gun from the glove compart-
ment and put it on the seat?
6. WITNESS: (1.5)
7. ATTORNEY: You don't know/that do you?
8. WITNESS: Not to my/knowledge I don't
9. ATTORNEY: One way or the other?
10. WITNESS: No.
11 ATTORNEY: All right you understand our question
and one way or the other you don't *know*
if it happened?
12. WITNESS: No sir I do not.
13. ATTORNEY: It could have happened?
14. WITNESS: (7.0) In *this* case?
15. ATTORNEY: It could have happened?
16. WITNESS: But I don't know – yes sir.
17. ATTORNEY: Thank you.

The witness, a police detective, asserts his inability to recall
whether any other officers got into the car in question before he
did. He recollects *some* details from the scene, however, noting
that there were other officers at the car, something presupposed
in the attorney's prior question. Nonetheless, the officer's
memory is claimed by him to fail on exactly the point which the

attorney is seeking to establish. (Utterance 4).

In such circumstances, an attorney is confronted with a set of options. There are no situatedly available procedures for establishing the veracity of the officer's claimed failure to recollect: even if this witness were to be led into a self-contradiction through further testimony, it could always be claimed (although perhaps with decreasing credibility) that his memory had suddenly been 'refreshed', and casting doubts upon *other* claims cannot serve determinately to demonstrate that everything said has been a lie or self-serving half-truth. This particular attorney, instead of seeking to discredit the witness's claim, chooses to bring to the fore the peculiar character of what is logically entailed by such an instance of forgetting: he seeks to show that an event that is forgotten stands equivalently as possibly having occurred as well as possibly not having occurred, and then moves to stress the former possibility. (Utterances 13 and 15).

A similar situation arises in the following extract, drawn from the Scarman Tribunal inquiry into the events in Northern Ireland:[6]

1. COUNSEL: Did you open the conversation with the Head Constable?
2. WITNESS: At this point in time I think I did. In my sort of recollection I think I did.
3. COUNSEL: Was there not talk about strangers in the flats?
4. WITNESS: Not to my knowledge. I cannot remember that at all. I did say that we wanted to get injured people out.
5. COUNSEL: Do you not recollect saying that there were strangers in the flat and that they were worried about getting out because they believed the police to be waiting for them at Pound Street?
6. WITNESS: No, I cannot remember that.
7. COUNSEL: Could you have said it?
8. WITNESS: I could have said that people wanted out.

Here, the item claimed as forgotten is something proposed as having been said by the witness himself in the presence of another (the Head Constable). Again, note that *some* details from the scene are recollected, and stand in contrast to the version being proposed by the Counsel. In Utterance 7, the Counsel deploys a similar interrogatory strategy as that shown in the previous extract: following a claim not to be able to remember something, it is the Interrogator's procedure to get on record that this is fully consistent with its possibly having occurred in just the way the interrogator has formulated it.

People are, on various occasions, expected to be able to recall, or *not* to have forgotten, certain sorts of details of their past experiences. The basis for such expectations is a common-sense presupposition about what *should* have been relevant, noticed, attended to, in a given scene or setting. To have forgotten certain matters can lead to being held responsible not (merely) for a 'cognitive malfunction' but for a *moral* lapse. This intertwining of the 'psychological' and the normative is much neglected in extant memory models, but appears at once when materials taken from everyday life are examined.

A recurrent difficulty which attends the production of a claim to have forgotten some called-for detail in a direct or cross examination is the management of a possible subsequent charge of evasion. Such a claim is open to attributions of strategic intent, depending upon its placement in a sequence of recollections, and may be taken to be an evasive gambit. In consequence, someone who comes up with such a claim to have forgotten may on occasion preface the claim with a disclaimer of any such strategic intent:[7]

Q: And where did you then put the gun?
A: I know this sounds strange, but I honestly can't remember.

The forgetting of certain kinds of things can occasion a demand for an excuse or justification; *entitled* forgettings form a particular domain constituted as such by the structure of the occasion within which the forgetting is available and by the normative assessment of the topical relevance of the forgotten detail within it.

3 'THOUGHT' AVOWALS AS SEQUENTIAL AND ILLOCUTIONARY OPERATORS

Whereas second- and third-person ascriptions of 'thoughts' (e.g., 'He (had the) thought that', 'You thought of it too late', 'She thought about it for a while', etc.) are rather transparently based upon public displays (speech, conduct, circumstances) for their warrantability, it is not so obvious what kinds of matters inform *first-person* employments (i.e., avowals), and they can easily be conceived of in theoretical reflection as all of one piece in reporting upon private mental occurrences on the part of the speaker.

In his unpublished writings, the late Harvey Sacks addressed himself to a class of locutions which included such *pre-announcement* forms as: 'I just had a thought'. He observed that:

> it happens that the thoughts, remembrances, wonderings and the like that persons have who are engaged in topical talk will routinely be on topic, and they exhibit that they are operating, absorbed in the talk, by presenting their talk with just such specific 'on topic' topic markers as 'I just wondered', 'I just remembered', 'I just had a thought', and the like.[8]

Sacks invites us to consider the following extract:

A: Um I just had a thought. I know someone who um uh has two smaller children, and uh would like, I think to get in some – just some weekends you know, but whether um she could do it regularly or no =
B: = Well =
A: = I think I'll talk to her.

He notes that the locution: 'I just had a thought' as it works here, positioned as a turn-initial component, marks the subsequent components as indeed on topic where they may otherwise not have appeared on topic. The pre-announcement here, then, can operate as a speaker's sequential operator for indicating that an up-coming announcement is going to unfold into one which is indeed topically relevant.

Sacks's insight here can be broadened considerably to show that such a construction can have conventional communicative functions and thus conventional modes of 'uptake' on the part of recipients, and I take it as a point of considerable significance that one does *not* find (joking contexts apart) such an 'uptake' as: 'Are you sure that it was a thought you just had?' or 'How do you know it was a sudden thought?' or 'Are you sure you translated that thought properly into words?' On various models of what 'thoughts' are, any one of these modes of uptake would be theoretically appropriate, and yet it is clear that their *actual* production in talk would be intelligible only as a feature of joking or, as Wittgenstein wryly noted, of a certain sort of metaphysical philosophy.

A query such as, 'Are you sure?' may well be appropriately placed following an avowal of one of the *achievement-verbs* in our mental vocabulary, such as: 'I *understand* what you're saying', or 'I *remember* it now', or 'I *know* it was him' again depending upon context, without any joking intention assignable to it. However, following a thought-avowal of the kind referred to, no such query has a proper place without signalling a (perhaps deliberately) deviant hearing of its function. If thought-avowals *did* conventionally function as reports upon inner goings-on in such cases, then the accuracy or correctness of the reports could logically be subject to question on at least some occasion and would be orientable-to as a serious inquiry. But this is not the way in which they work.

Let us consider some other illocutionary functions of 'I thought' plus an optional complementiser ('that') plus a subordinate clause. Perhaps the principal use of this locution is to signal *either* a 'guardedness' with respect to some object-complement (expressed in the subordinate clause), *or* a current recognition that what had previously been held to be the case (guardedly or otherwise) is now clearly *not* the case.[9] Sacks has pointed out that the use in story formats of 'I thought (that)' plus an object-complement can orient the hearer to the prospective but so-far unannounced failure already known to the speaker; i.e., when someone is telling a story or producing an extended

account and comes up with 'I thought X', by and large they are
saying that now it turns out not to be so in the way you are about
to hear.[10] However, there is at least *one* set of uses of 'I thought
that' plus an object-complement (characteristically stressing
'thought') in which a very similar function is fulfilled as would be
the case were 'I knew that' to be used in its place. Consider the
following scenario. Someone arrives at a party about whose
coming there were some grounds for doubt but whose coming was
perhaps hoped-for. On his or her arrival, the host greets with the
expression: 'I *thought* you'd make it!'' thus signalling the
(appreciated?) confirmation of an expectation or hope.[11]

So far, we have confined our attention to 'thoughts *that*'. We
must now consider 'thoughts *of*' and 'thoughts *about*', two
constructions most immediately amenable to incorporation into
a version of 'mental report prefaces'. Thoughts of or about some
object-complement are characteristically taken to be images,
mental picturings or silent soliloquies, and their avowals to be
reports of or about such occurrences. As noted earlier, we do not
need to deny the obvious that there are indeed such phenomena
as 'mental picturings' and 'silent monologues'. However, it is
crucial to keep in mind that no image, sequence of images nor
silent soliloquy taken by itself, apart from some particular (social)
context, determines what thought(s) it expresses. Any image,
sequence of images or silent soliloquy can, in different contexts,
express different thoughts of or about something. There is no
necessarily invariant relationship between what any given
thought (*of* or *about*) something amounts to and the images or
words which express it. Moreover, we should be wary of attribut-
ing to *all* locutions, in which such expressions as 'I thought of' and
'I thought about' are employed, one single unitary function of
reporting. Indeed, we should take note of a genuine peculiarity of
such locutions, a peculiarity which marks them off significantly
from all other instances properly referred to as 'reports'. Unlike
other types of reports, *these* reports (if that is how we are to
conceive of at least one aspect of their illocutionary force)
uniformly depend for their truth upon the truthfulness of the
avowing agent. For other reports, a speaker may be speaking

truthfully in offering them, but he could still be mistaken, wrong, inaccurate or simply deceived. For the set of 'reports' using 'I thought of' or 'I thought about' plus an object-complement, it seems usually to be the truthfulness of the disclosing agent that warrants the truth accorded to them and it is unintelligible to doubt the veracity of the 'report' without *eo ipso* doubting the sincerity with which it was/is being offered. Wittgenstein remarked:

> The criteria for the truth of the *confession* that I thought such-and-such are not the criteria for a true *description* of a process. And the importance of the true confession does not reside in its being a correct and certain report of a process. It resides rather in the special consequences which can be drawn from a confession whose truth is guaranteed by the special criteria of *truthfulness*.[12]

Of course, not all instances of use of 'I thought of' and 'I thought about' along with their object-complements express 'inner' soliloquies etc. Often, they may be used to communicate a wholly public matter, as when I say that I thought of a solution to the problem when what I did was abruptly to state it in a meeting, or when what I did was to discuss it with my wife. Here, some (potentially) public events can be called upon to justify, or to establish the veracity of, my report. They can be invoked to defeat my claim, as well. But what could be appealed to in defeating a claim to have thought of or about something silently or privately?

In some cases where a silent thought is publicly disclosed, there is a detail which can be corrected by an interlocutor. I say to my colleague, who has asked me what I am doing, that I am sitting thinking about the Dean's speech to the faculty yesterday, and he tells me that the Dean's speech was made the day before. I reply to him that of course he is right, and perhaps add that it made such an impression on me that it seemed as if it had been yesterday when he spoke. With the detail corrected, and in the absence of any further non-corroborating contextual particulars, I am accorded full sovereignty over my avowal. In cases in which my thought-avowal contains ratifiable/defeasible details, I can indeed be brought to acknowledge an error, a mistake in how I reported upon my silent thoughts. I could *not* have been thinking about the Dean's speech given yesterday because the Dean did not speak yesterday but the day before, when I was present and actually heard it. However, there are clearly *limits to retreat.* I can acknowledge only so much in the way of other-initiated correction to my thought-avowals before I may become subject to the suspicion that I was being untruthful in the avowal itself, and not merely wrong about some incidental details. And, naturally, what goes for me also goes for others in this matter.

In this discussion, I have said nothing about first-person employments of the present-tense form, 'think (that, of, about, in, up, on, etc.)' plus an object-complement. Uses of 'I think' conventionally signal that the object-complement is to be heard as an opinion, conclusion or judgment. Thus, 'I think (that)' may be treated, broadly, as a tentativeness marker which implicitly acknowledges either the defeasibility of what is being said or claimed, or the relative uncertainty of the speaker with respect to it. 'I think' is not a descriptive or referential expression of any kind. In this domain of first-person 'psychological' expressions, then, there is less of a temptation to construe their operative features as if they were mental 'observational terms'. And it is that temptation which I have been trying here to undermine.

4 SENSATION CONCEPTUALISATION AND 'INCORRIGIBILITY'

So far, these study sketches have focused upon the interactive constitution and management of such 'cognitive' particulars (I do not say 'phenomena' advisedly) as 'intending', 'forgetting' and 'thought'. In this discussion, I shall concentrate upon the interactive constitution and management of an experiential predicate, 'pain', which has been the topic of a large literature in both the philosophy of mind and epistemology as well as in the behavioural sciences.

One recurrent view of 'pain' is that, with the exception of borderline cases between which one may have trouble figuring out what to say, in the normal range of cases someone who avows having a pain is the sole and incorrigible authority as to its nature. Such a version of pain-avowals is clearly adequate for characterising many common sequences of their occurrence, as in the ensuing transcript from a doctor – patient encounter:[13]

1. DOCTOR: (   ) And Sunday evening it was where when it started?
2. PATIENT: On the right
3. DOCTOR: On the right side there
4. PATIENT: Yes
5. DOCTOR: And it's sharp pain when you get it?
6. PATIENT: Well, it's been varying. At times it's sharp and then at times it's sort of a dull ache.
7. DOCTOR: Uh huh. And it comes and goes through the day?
8. PATIENT: No it it'll come on and stay for about two hours and then leave.
9. DOCTOR: Is it related to your –
10. PATIENT: Doesn't seem to be related to food.

The patient is, throughout this sequence, treated as the authority on the location and nature of his pain as well as its periodicity of occurrence. This stands in clear contrast to many other matters relating to the patient's condition about which the doctor assumes definitional responsibility.

An initial observation about the perfectly routine and normal series of 'references to pain' is that the patient, in Utterance 6. asserts its variability to the extent that he invokes not only the contrasting descriptors 'sharp' and 'dull', but even a new substantive, 'ache', whilst sustaining his reference to 'it' as an invariant under these transformations. This pronoun ties back to the physician's use in Utterance 5. of the expression 'sharp pain'. It appears, then, that the patient is speaking of the *same* thing when, in some other context, one may draw a distinction *between* a 'pain' and an 'ache' and speak of them as quite different things, or a distinction between a sharp pain and a dull one as different pains. Here, it appears that the fundamental criterion for the individuation of pain is not tonal quality but location ('on the right side there').

We do not conventionally have any purpose for challenging or altering the ways in which someone (e.g., a patient) articulates his or her pains and this fact can blind us to the negotiability of first-person pain-avowals. Consider the following cases, brought to light by my colleague W.T. Anderson during the course of his extensive research into dentist-patient relations and inter-actions:[14]

1. DENTIST: . . . you really shouldn't be that sore there
   (0.5)
2. PATIENT: Maybe I'm just a little uh:
3. DENTIST: You might be
4. PATIENT: I – maybe it's a lot psychological like that
5. DENTIST: Okay
6. PATIENT: I kn- I think they hurt and they probably
   don't even hurt that much =
7. DENTIST: = All right.

In this case, the dentist's suggestion that the patient ought not be 'that sore there' is acted upon in a process of step-wise down-grading of what had been an initial pain-reaction to the point of near extinction. Elsewhere, dentists can be found proposing candidate sensation-descriptors to patients who then pick them up and use them in first-person avowals, as in:[15]

1. DENTIST: Feel any tingling up there
   (.............)
5. DENTIST: Is it creeping up anywhere!
   (.............)
30. PATIENT: Not much more no. It hasn't really creeped
   into it.
   (.............)

88. PATIENT: YEAH, much better (.) this is pretty numb
    now (.) it's *ting*ling up here.

The dentist is the first to introduce the descriptors 'tingling'
and 'creeping', and they are appropriated by the patient to
conceptualise his sensations. Anderson points out that in these
ways, dentists can and do manage tolerable expressions of
sensation in their surgeries, usually in the direction of
minimisation.[16]

In case anyone is still unsure about the degree to which
personal, 'subjective' sensations are amenable, in various interactional contexts, to interactive negotiation and constitution, the
following (final) example should serve as a corrective. In this
instance, a self-ascription of *death* was seriously made *in spite of* the
persistence of consciousness and sentience:[17]

> Despite wounds in his heart and lungs, he said, he was able to
> run to a hospital . . . He was taken [after collapsing – JC] in a
> stretcher across the street to the emergency room.
>   'I felt myself slipping out but I had a determination to live',
> he said. 'The hardest part was that I couldn't breathe. I heard
> them saying, "I can't feel no pulse, I can't feel no pulse." I
> could hear them keep saying that'.
>   'I said, "that's it. I'm gone." I just knew I was dead.'

5 CONCLUDING REMARKS

In one of his last published writings, Theodore Mischel surveyed
the state of the psychology of 'the self'.[18] He argued that, to those
who are familiar with 'Wittgensteinian arguments pertaining to the
necessity of supplying outer criteria for "inner states" ', a
programme of empirical research which attempts to 'abstract the
social context and "look inside" instead', in a move to discrimin-
ate internal inner states or unconscious, internal 'controlling
variables' for conduct, is unlikely to pass muster. For Mischel,
'concepts like belief, intention and the rest . . . are also part of a

conceptual system – the one we normally use to make our own behaviour and that of others intelligible'. He then made the following proposal:

> The business of tidying and tightening the complex inter-relations between these concepts and the criteria for their deployment, of developing and checking out analyses which this conceptual system suggests, of determining the boundaries of its application, and the like, could be a properly scientific task for a social science.[19]

I am in sympathy with this general approach to the study of mind and conduct, but would like to draw attention to a basic point of divergence. In Mischel's argument, the social scientist interested in these topics is urged to respect the pre-existing conceptual structures of everyday life, but is then told to set about 'tidying and tightening' them, presumably in the interest of theory construction. Although this is far from a directive to 'operationalise' in the (unsatisfactory) old way, there remains a quite unnecessarily stipulative element in his proposal. In my view, as I have sought to elaborate it here (and elsewhere), the prospects for genuinely rigorous theory construction in the non-biological human sciences remain open, but must surely be constrained by the minutest attention to the detailed and mundane phenomena of conduct if we are to avoid the pitfalls of the tradition that we are trying to overcome. If a theory of conduct, in any of its aspects, is to be truly disciplined, then it must yield statements which actually deliver on the properties of the phenomena under scrutiny, and not continue to indulge in (arbitrary) idealisations and model-building far from the particulars of actual, naturally-occurring domains of real behaviour in the everyday world in which we actually live. The elucidation of the properties of practical action and reasoning, of the human conceptual apparatus as it is actually put to work, buttressed by empirical detail to which we must remain fully responsive, is in itself a sufficient task for a 'scientific social science' in Mischel's sense.

One consideration that emerges from the sort of work I have exemplified here is that any theory of mind – when we are in a position to construct one, which at present is not the case – is going to form a part of a theory of social conduct and social conceptualisation, and perhaps not even a major component of it. Moreover, it is highly unlikely that any non-trivial theory whose empirical propositions are isomorphic with the phenomena it treats will take the form of a deductive-nomological scheme or set of laws. Why should it? If we take a careful look at ethnomethodo logical research over the past ten years or so, I think that we will find that its most successful and sophisticated theoretical contribution – the construction of a rigorous model of human interactive co-ordination articulated in the 'Simplest Systematics for Turn-Taking'[20] – required a good deal of patient study of transcribed, naturally-occurring sequences of interpersonal communication. And its formal structure was much more akin to a recursive rule-set than to any sort of 'predictive' model.

In the present context, we are at least in a position to benefit from the careful, piecemeal work done in analytical and linguistic philosophy on the logical grammar of mental and related concepts, predicates and expressions. In many ways, what is recommended here (and to some extent presupposed in Mischel's programme) is to build upon that work and turn it towards the elucidation, not of hypothetical cases exclusively, but of actual empirical materials. The goals may turn out to be dissimilar, but the heuristic of attempting to discern an 'informal' logic in human dealings with the mental, the experiential, the subjective, is a fruitful starting-point. And surely, a fresh start *is* required. It is going to take the intellectual labours of many to realise whatever potential there is in a programme that breaks with behaviourism and mentalism (including the neo-mentalism of the cognitivists), but which still insists that an abstract, interesting and empirically grounded study of cognition is possible.

NOTES

1. J. Coulter, *The Social Construction of Mind* (London: Macmillan, 1979).
2. Although I cannot document this assertion with transcribed materials, such an occurrence became quite common in the work of the psychiatric social workers with whom I conducted my researches.
3. James M. Henslin, 'Guilt and Guilt Neutralization: Response and Adjustment to Suicide' in Jack D. Douglas (ed.), *Deviance and Respectability: The Social Construction of Moral Meanings* (Irvine, Calif.: Basic Books, 1970).
4. Steinar Kvale, 'The Temporality of Memory', *Journal of Phenomenological Psychology*, vol. 5, no. 1, Fall 1974, p. 24.
5. Amy Neustein, *Courtroom Examination: An Analysis of Its Formal Properties*, Unpublished doctoral dissertation, Sociology, Boston University, 1981.
6. From the Official Transcripts of the Scarman Tribunal Hearings into Violence and Civil Disorder in Northern Ireland, 1969.
7. Extract supplied by Shera Jarvis, to whom I am grateful.
8. Harvey Sacks, *Aspects of the Sequential Organization of Conversation*, University of California at Irvine: unpublished MSS., n.d., p. 19.
9. For a fuller discussion of these properties of the use of 'thought', see my *The Social Construction of Mind*, ch. 5.
10. Harvey Sacks, *Transcribed Lectures* (University of California at Irvine, 1970). Sacks here described the 'first-verb' property of invocations of 'thought' in accounts of events, noting that a typical 'second' verb would be 'realised' or 'found out' (otherwise than had been thought).
11. I am indebted to Anne Rawls for this observation.
12. Ludwig Wittgenstein, *Philosophical Investigations*, trans. G.E.M. Anscombe (Oxford: Basil Blackwell, 1968) p. 222.
13. I am indebted to the Boston University Interaction Research Group for the use of this transcript.
14. W.T. Anderson, *Behavior in Painful Places: Aspects of the Dentist-Patient Encounter*, Unpublished doctoral dissertation, Department of Sociology, Boston University, 1982. I am most grateful to Tim Anderson for his kind permission to use these extracts, as well as for hours of stimulating discussion over the years.
15. Ibid., p. 177, and pp. 179–80.
16. W.T. Anderson (personal communication), 1982.
17. *New York Times*, Sunday, December 28, 1980. I am indebted to Lena Jayyusi who discovered this marvellous extract.
18. Theodore Mischel, 'Conceptual Issues in the Psychology of the Self' in his edited collection, *The Self: Psychological and Philosophical Issues* (Oxford: Basil Blackwell, 1977).
19. Ibid., p. 18. Previous quotations from p. 13 and p. 17.
20. H. Sacks, E.A. Schegloff and G. Jefferson, 'A Simplest Systematics for the Organisation of Turn-Taking for Conversation', *Language*, vol. 50, no. 4, Part 1, December 1974.

8 On the dereification of mind

Although I believe that the arguments presented in this work point toward the possibility of a principled distinction between the study of mind (as properly conceived) and the study of brains and nervous systems, it is quite obvious that without the necessary physiological equipment to enable us to do what we do (so that the mental vocabulary can apply to us) there would be nothing for the student of mind to study. The main point being advanced here is that because the mental vocabulary is governed by a practical logic, originating within and having its proper locus within the 'natural attitude' of mundane social life, it does not consist in proper 'natural kind designators' which could be used to locate phenomena for which adequate physiological explanations might be sought. Moreover, due to the irreducibility of the predicates of meaningful action to strict behavioural event predicates, it seems clear that the vocabulary of conduct in general has this same property.

In this concluding discussion, I want to outline some of the problems which have arisen in psychophysiological research and theorising when components from an essentially vernacular, ascriptive set of categories are utilised as research-guiding concepts. In earlier chapters, I have mentioned some of the difficulties that arise when concepts such as 'memory', 'decision-making', 'think' – even 'behaving' – are implicitly treated as natural-kind concepts rather than complex, polymorphous family-resemblance concepts, or are subject to generalised criticism on the grounds that they are not 'good enough' natural-kind concepts. Here, I shall consider two polar concepts, 'schizophrenia' and 'intelligence', and try to demonstrate some of the fundamental perplexities that have arisen when they are

147

hypostatised within psychophysiological research programmes. The argument will not be that the problems arise because these are somehow 'inadequate' concepts, but that their proper domain of functioning is elsewhere, and the difficulties encountered with their use in research contexts are attributable not to their putatively general deficiencies as concepts but to the erroneous attempt to transpose them into inappropriate domains of application.

1 'SCHIZOPHRENIA' AS A NATURAL KIND

In a comprehensive study published in the *Schizophrenia Bulletin*,[1] Joseph H. Stephens reviewed the situation in respect of diagnostic reliability for the 'schizophrenias', discussing the findings of, *inter alia*, Wing, Cooper and Sartorius,[2] A.A. Stone *et al.*,[3] M.M. Katz *et al.*,[4] Brill and Glass,[5] R.A. Munoz *et al.*,[6] W.T. Carpenter Jnr *et al.*[7] and R.E. Kendell.[8] Noting that 'the subdivision of schizophrenia into paranoid, hebephrenic, catatonic and simple has not proved particularly useful'[9] in guiding attempts at formulating standardised diagnostic manuals and diagnostic practices, he adds that most researchers 'emphasise the generally unsatisfactory classification of schizophrenia and the need for a more meaningful nomenclature'.[10] In particular, he draws upon the study by Kendell to suggest that:

> The characteristic features of any given condition usually do not have to be present in order to establish the diagnosis. To be diagnosed as schizophrenic, in common practice, a patient does not have to possess all of the typical symptoms of schizophrenia but only some of them . . . . Textbooks usually provide general descriptions of typical features of syndromes rather than criteria for establishing their presence.'[11]

This situation has not appreciably changed since Bannister's classic paper on the logic of research into schizophrenia,[12] in which he noted that the category could not be used to generate any uniform or internally homogeneous sample of cases suitable for nomothetic research of an etiological or epidemiological kind. It is little surprise, then, to find researchers such as Buchsbaum documenting the following:

> Pharmacologic and neurochemical investigations yield amazingly wide individual variation from schizophrenic to schizophrenic. This individual variation may be taken as indicating that the variable under investigation is not being measured properly or is irrelevant to schizophrenia. It may also indicate that a wide variety of neurochemical or neuro-physiological bases underlie the schizophrenic syndrome.[13]

He adds that a 'biologically homogeneous sub-group' has been 'elusive'.[14] Kety, in a detailed discussion of heredity and environment in schizophrenia (published in 1978, a year after Buchsbaum's paper), commented upon a study of adopted off-spring of diagnosed schizophrenic biological parents in these terms:

> we may be dealing not with a single illness but with a hetero-geneous cluster of illnesses that have different etiologies . . . . The best evidence that environmental factors are important comes from twin studies, which show that the concordance rate [for the diagnosis of schizophrenia – JC] among monozygotic twins is only fifty percent. Clearly, genetic factors alone cannot account for the whole story.[15]

I remember detailing similar arguments many years ago in order to support an *in-principle* position against the view that 'schizophrenia' was a genuine 'natural kind' category usable in serious research; I was told repeatedly that this was an extreme reaction to a transient state of affairs, and that as soon as the Present State Examination schedule and similar diagnostic codifications had been fairly checked out, all of my 'logical' arguments would evaporate as so much philosophical effluvia. However, not only has this not been borne out, there are no signs whatsoever that it ever could be. 'Schizophrenia' is an evaluative construct and a polymorph whose application criteria are contextually variable, a claim now commonplace in social psychology. Why, then, is there such a persistent professional adherence to what Klerman has termed 'a scientific nosology' which fails to question the usability of Bleuler's old notion in research contexts?[16]

I believe that at least a part of the answer to this question is to be found in the persistence of certain highly implausible assumptions about the mind, human conduct and the nature of 'behavioural pathologies' which are shared by many (prominent) advocates of positivistic epistemology in the study of these topics. The primary assumption appears to be that the ascription of a category such as 'schizophrenia' to someone amounts to the formulation of a scientific hypothesis about the presence of an 'underlying' state or condition for which the category serves as a name, by analogy to the way in which 'the fevers' were ascribed to persons who would now be diagnosed as tuberculous, choleric and so on.

Any actual inquiry into psychiatric *praxis* immediately casts doubt on this assumption. 'Symptoms' of mental illnesses for which no locus of physiological impairment can be found are not thereby recast as something else: they are *indefeasible* with respect to negative results on biochemical and physiological screenings, resulting in the peculiarity of the so-called 'functional psychoses' or 'non-organic mental disorders', which in turn can be appealed to for the rationalisation of the psychiatric labelling. 'Symptoms' are interactively available, contextually constituted forms of human conduct; they are available in 'functional' cases *in no other way*. In Goffman's elegant description, they

> directly express the whole array of divisive social alignments: alienation, rebellion, insolence, untrustworthiness, hostility, apathy, importunement, intrusiveness, and so forth.[17]

In addition, the deployment of a quasi-scientific vocabulary in attributions of this sort may relieve the attributor of some of the burden of moral judgment. For the patient, if he runs out of excuses or justifications for the performance of situatedly deviant actions (including the serious articulation of assignably deviant beliefs and/or perceptual accounts), the official ascription of schizophrenia can ultimately operate as an indefeasible excusing condition for him. Given such 'latent functions', to borrow Merton's celebrated expression, the price paid for reification of the complex of conduct-circumstances-assessment into a putative 'state' might not seem too high for practical purposes. The subsequent myth, which has it that 'schizophrenia' is a natural-kind term (like water, temperature or energy) for which all we require is an adequate operationalisation, can then get off the ground. The truth of the matter is that no meaningful operational definition(s) have been developed which correspond to anything but a fraction of the actual populations currently spending their time in mental hospitals under the auspices of the diagnostic category of 'schizophrenia'. In these circumstances, it is little cause of wonder that essentially irrational doctrines about the 'myth of mental illness' can get off the ground.

Let me state unequivocally that, whilst the proper sphere of application of categories such as those belonging to the set of functional mental disorders is a matter of intense moral struggle in everyday affairs, it is futile to suppose that there is 'no such thing as mental illness without a biological causation'. If we keep in mind the general equivalence of functional mental disorder with serious ascriptions of 'craziness', 'madness' and 'insanity', which are as mundanely applicable as any other ascriptive concepts for human behaviour, we will be less prepared to jettison this set of moral concepts than we might otherwise be. And, notwithstanding the contemporary mania for scientising our moral problems, we are ultimately confronted with our moral responsibilities in this domain: there is no refuge to be had within the essentially mystified realm of positivistic psychopathology, at least within its programmatic self-understanding.

In sum, the evidence which has been accumulating for some considerable time supports the contention that the reification of schizophrenia as an enduring, underlying 'state' of persons diagnosed as such (and shared with heterogeneous others) is a fallacy. It is a product of that unchecked nomothetic impulse derived from a version of theorising appropriate to medical, not behavioural, science.

2 'INTELLIGENCE' AS A NATURAL KIND

It was Boring who asserted that intelligence is what intelligence tests test. Since then, a variety of analogies with operationalism in the physical sciences have been appealed to in justifying the theoretical treatment of intelligence as if it were a generic term collecting discrete properties of persons. I.Q. tests are still being proposed as literal measures (albeit with diverse degrees of 'contamination' or 'bias' by the very factors which actually constitute our normative judgments, such as 'culture'!), and this is rationalised by an appeal to the practice of measuring heat by thermometers or electric charge by voltmeters. As Block and Dworkin put it in their discussion of the heritability controversy:

Many psychologists seem to have the impression that I.Q. has roughly the same relation to the ordinary notion of intelligence that Newton's concept of mass had to common seventeenth-century notions of mass. At the same time, many of them (Jensen and Herrnstein included) actually use 'smart', 'stupid', 'bright', 'dull', 'intelligent', 'unintelligent' in stylistic variation with 'high/low I.Q.'. They thereby transfer to I.Q. all the emotional and conceptual associations the reader has to intelligence. All this after we are disarmed by being told that after all, 'intelligence' is just a word like any other word, and how a scientist chooses to use it is just a matter of stipulation . . . . Given their practice of using 'I.Q.', interchangeably with 'intelligence', 'smartness', 'brightness', and so forth, it is somewhat surprising to find these psychologists deploring public misunderstandings of the psychometric use of the term 'intelligence'.[18]

This practice can be found even in some of the classic statements articulating important *caveats* about inferences from I.Q.
test scores, such as Hebb's. In the second edition of his widely
known textbook on psychology,[19] Hebb warns against 'nonsense'
statements such as: '80 per cent of intelligence is determined by
heredity, 20 per cent by environment',[20] and compares them to
more perspicuously absurd assertions sharing the same formal
structure. He notes that: 'asking how much heredity contributes
to man's intelligence is like asking how much the width of a field
contributes to its area, and how much its length contributes'[21]
where what we should say is that both are 100 per cent important;
the relation is not additive but multiplicative. However, the inter-
changeability of 'intelligence' with 'I.Q.' still permeates Hebb's
reasoning, as in remarks such as the following: 'if then there was
no significant difference in I.Q., we could not conclude that
intelligence is unaffected by the sensory environment.'[22]

The conception of intelligence which appears to inform these
illicit identifications is one in which it is tacitly construed as a state
descriptor for which the 'state' is conjectured to be an unobservable condition of the person. This underlying and enduring
attribute – the 'intelligence' of the person – is thought of as an
evolving and eventually stabilising property of his mind or brain
which generates conduct and dispositions that give us only the
most tenuous clues about it. I.Q. tests are needed (and here we
ignore their purely pragmatic employment for non-theoretical
purposes by, e.g., school administrators for streaming children)
because it is only by concentrating a series of mundanely
acknowledged 'tasks requiring intelligence' into a relatively brief
time period that a researcher can aspire to determine the
'amount' of intelligence which a person has. It is not too difficult
to see that the subsequent equation of test scores, summed up in
a quotient, with someone's 'amount of' or 'level of' intelligence
is one of the purest cases of a scientific artefact masquerading as
a finding. Blumer put it very nicely:

Intelligence is seen in empirical life as present in such varied
things as the skilful military planning of an army general, the

ingenious exploitation of a market situation by an entrepreneur, effective methods of survival by a disadvantaged slum dweller, the clever meeting of the problems of his world by a peasant or primitive tribesman, the cunning of low-grade delinquent girl morons in a detention home, and the construction of telling verse by a poet. It should be immediately clear how ridiculous and unwarranted it is to believe that the operationalising of intelligence through a given intelligence test yields a satisfactory picture of intelligence.[23]

Let us shift the focus of the discussion to a closely related matter. There is a strong temptation, when reflecting upon the meaning of 'intelligent conduct', to think that it is 'intelligence' (construed, as noted, as an underlying mental condition of some kind) which *makes* the conduct intelligent. The underlying 'intelligence' can then become a topic for speculative psychological hypotheses about its 'realisation' in the nervous system, about its 'causative powers', and so on.

Fodor's discussion of 'clever clowning', taking the example from Ryle's famous discussion,[24] is a case in point. Ryle had been concerned to argue that the 'cleverness' of the clown's clowning did not consist in its being the surface effects of deep, interior mental causes but rather in its being, *inter alia*, amusing to his audience, involving unexpected moves, and comprised of actions of various sorts justifiably seen as witty, humorous, etc., in their context of production. It is clear that Ryle's discussion was intended to show how vernacular attributions of predicates like 'clever' and 'intelligent' depend not upon some occult divinations of the interiors of people but upon public criteria in actual circumstances of conduct. Whatever may be going on inside the clown when his clowning is clever cannot sensibly be called the 'operation of intelligence' which somehow 'produces' his behaviour. The 'operation of one's intelligence' is displayed, is available, *in* situated conduct open to assessment in such terms.

Fodor quite wrongly reads all of this as an exemplification of something he calls 'logical behaviorism', i.e., the doctrine that all mental concepts and predicates yield to logical analysis in terms of statements of necessary and sufficient behavioural conditions for their application (with the familiar equivocation as to whether 'actions' fall under the category of the 'behavioural'). Yet nowhere has Ryle asserted that his list of the criteria which make the clown's clowning clever was an approximation to what could eventually become a precise *set* of behavioural conditions, and such conditions alone. Ryle's view was more akin to Wittgenstein's on this matter (although here and there he does come closer to a logical regimentation of the mental vocabulary: *vide* his treatment of 'having a motive'). But this is not the heart of the matter. Fodor wants to construe the question: 'What *makes* the clown's clowning clever? or 'What *causes* the clown's pratfall to be witty?' not only as a *conceptual* one but also as a *nomological* one (i.e., what internal events in the clown generated the conduct describable as clever or witty). He claims that '*both* the causal *and* the conceptual story can be simultaneously true, distinct answers to questions of the form: 'What makes (an) *x* (an) *F*?'[25] It is this move, involving as it does an idiosyncratic reading of 'makes' and 'causes' in the Rylean example, which, he seems to believe, undermines Ryle's case. That case, it will be remembered, was exactly that such a transposition of the meaning of such expressions in such contexts can produce an incoherent causal metaphysics of the mental.[26]

Although Fodor is too sophisticated a thinker to argue that concepts such as 'intelligent' and 'clever' are state descriptors whose referents are unobservable, inner phenomena, his reasoning here is strikingly similar to that which is embodied in the claim that there is something *behind* some line(s) of conduct which is what gives that conduct its character as 'intelligent'. Ryle's (correct) answer to this kind of position is simply to deny the intelligibility of its entailments; the intelligence is *in* the behaviour-in-context, there for anyone to see, and were it not publicly available our ordinary use of the word would be very different and it becomes hard to imagine how its use might have been learned by speakers of the ordinary language. Yet someone who denies that what gives conduct its status as 'intelligent' is something internal to the person is easily subject to the wholly mistaken accusation that he is denying the causal efficacy of the brain or central nervous system. The two points are quite unrelated to each other. If brain events *do* cause bodily movements in some mechanistic sense, then it is still neither the brain events nor the resultant bodily movements which give intelligent conduct its character *as* intelligent: it is the behaviour *in addition to, or in the context of*, criterial circumstances and appraisals of it.

These problems of conceptualisation arise repeatedly because of what I can only describe as an irrational but entrenched prejudice among their proponents against grasping the *sociological* dimension of human conduct. I venture this remark with some trepidation, not least because I am a professional sociologist with an interest in advancing the intellectual domains of my discipline; charges of academic imperialism lurk around us! However, there is no reason whatsoever why academic psychology has to ignore the socio-cultural, any more than sociology has to ignore the human biological constitution. The study of human action, inter-action and reasoning cannot be compartmentalised adequately without a thorough appreciation of the actual relationships obtaining between cognition, conduct and culture: the difficulties outlined here derive from failing to deal with this pressing and foundational problem in a way that is uncluttered by *a priori* allegiances to fetishised disciplinary boundaries and defective philosophies of science.

3 METAPHORS AND MIND

I want to conclude this chapter by insisting upon a distinction between two sorts of metaphors in scientific work. The first sort I shall call *metaphors of cogent assimilation*, and the second sort I shall call *unwarranted transpositions*.

The hydrodynamical model for electrical theory may be cited as a good example of the use of metaphor in the cogent assimilation of disparate phenomena (water and electricity). Indeed, so productive was the employment of this metaphor that its initially metaphorical status may be said to have waned as we naturally express ourselves about electrical phenomena in terms of 'flow', 'current' and so forth. There are many other such examples in the history of science, and the many successes have inspired behavioural scientists to attempt to make similar moves. The abiding problem remains that most such efforts have resulted in unwarranted transpositions which have seriously hindered inquiry by blocking a better understanding of the *a priori* conceptual constitution of the phenomena of interest, be they human acts, mental states or pathological conditions.

One quite central metaphorical construction illustrative of the problem in the behavioural sciences is that of the 'unconscious'. From the Freudian hydraulics of mind to the contemporary computational analogy, the result has been to personify the mind or brain and to lose the person in the process. There is, of course, nothing wrong at all in saying that someone did something unconsciously (meaning: pre-reflectively, habitually, without thinking, or spontaneously). Problems arise, however, when either (i) actions are assigned, or motives, desires, thoughts, etc., are imputed to persons in the absence of ordinary ascription criteria and are claimed nonetheless to have a 'locus' in the unconscious 'mind' of the persons in question, or (ii) mundane activities are uniformly construed as the outputs of some internal programming operative out of the awareness of those engaged in the activities. (The latter device is postulated often as a psychologist's equivalent to the notion of a brain code postulated in certain neurophysiological models of sensory processing: a denial of the former is sometimes taken to amount to a denial of the latter, quite without warrant as far as I can see.)

A major impetus to defend the theoretical status of a notion like 'the unconscious' arises from an instrumentalist view of theoretical concepts. (Philosophical realists have a harder time with this notion, and occasionally, following Freud himself, appeal to the physical brain as the 'real' locus of the unconscious which itself is then articulated as a sort of 'provisionally abstract description' of brain functions. This is a peculiar move – for what is an 'abstract description' of brain functions other than a description of how it works in general terms, something for which no additional notion of an 'unconscious mind' is at all necessary?) What, then, is 'instrumentalism' in this context? From what I can gather, we are being asked to tolerate the theoretical and research-guiding use of a concept on the assumption that, via its use, increasingly predictive explanations of human behaviour will be forthcoming. The best that one can presently say about this in connection with the role of appeals to 'unconscious *mental* states and processes' in behavioural science is that nothing of the kind has occurred. Instead, we are moving further and further away from the proper object of the study of man: man himself, as he conducts his life in social settings.

NOTES

1. J.H. Stephens, 'Long-Term Prognosis and Follow-up in Schizophrenia', *Schizophrenia Bulletin* (N.I.M.H.), vol. 4, no. 1, 1978.
2. J.K. Wing, J.E. Cooper and N. Sartorius, *The Measurement and Classification of Psychiatric Symptoms* (Cambridge: Cambridge University Press, 1974).
3. A.A. Stone, R. Hopkins, M.W. Mahnke, D.W. Shapiro and H.A. Silvergate, 'Simple Schizophrenia: Syndrome or Shibboleth?' *American Journal of Psychiatry*, vol. 125, 1968.
4. M.M. Katz, J.O. Cole and H.A. Lowery, 'Non-specificity of Diagnosis of Paranoid Schizophrenia', *Archives of General Psychiatry*, vol. 11, 1964.
5. N.Q. Brill and J.F. Glass, 'Hebephrenic Schizophrenic Reactions', *Archives of General Psychiatry*, vol. 12, 1965.
6. R.A. Munoz, G. Kulak, S. Marten and V.B. Tuason, 'Simple and Hebephrenic Schizophrenia: A Follow-up Study' in M. Roff, L.N. Robins and M. Pollack (eds), *Life History Research in Psychopathology, vol. 2* (Minneapolis: University of Minnesota Press, 1972).
7. W.T. Carpenter Jnr., J.J. Bartko, C.L. Carpenter and J.S. Strauss, 'Another View of Schizophrenic Subtypes', *Archives of General Psychiatry*, vol. 33, 1976.
8. R.E. Kendell, *The Role of Diagnosis in Psychiatry* (Oxford: Blackwell Scientific Publications, 1975).
9. J.H. Stephens, 'Schizophrenia', p. 28.
10. Ibid.
11. Ibid.
12. D. Bannister, 'The Logical Requirements for Research into Schizophrenia', *British Journal of Psychiatry*, vol. 114, 1968.
13. Monte S. Buchsbaum, 'Psychophysiology and Schizophrenia', *Schizophrenia Bulletin*, vol. 3, no. 1, 1977, p. 12.
14. Ibid.

15. Seymour Kety, 'Heredity and Environment' in John C. Shershow (ed.), *Schizophrenia: Science and Practice* (Cambridge, Mass.: Harvard University Press, 1978) p. 60. Cf. Kety, 'Prospects for Research in Schizophrenia: An Overview' in Francis O. Schmitt, George Adelman and Frederic G. Worden (eds), *Neurosciences Research Symposium Summaries, vol. 7* (Cambridge, Mass.: M.I.T. Press, 1973) p. 460 and *passim*.

16. Gerald L. Klerman, 'The Evolution of a Scientific Nosology' in Shershow (ed.) *Schizophrenia*; Klerman attacks the 'labeling school of sociology and social psychology', mentioning Scheff and Rosenhan, but does not go into details. I think that he misses the point of sociological research into the ascription of insanity and its implications for his 'scientific nosology', although the analysis of labelling practices does not amount to a genuine *theory* of schizophrenia at all.

17. Erving Goffman, 'The Insanity of Place' in his *Relations in Public* (New York: Basic Books, 1971), p. 387.

18. N.J. Block and Gerald Dworkin, 'I.Q., Heritability and Inequality' in N.J. Block and Gerald Dworkin (eds), *The I.Q. Controversy* (New York: Pantheon Books, Random House, 1976), p. 429.

19. D.O. Hebb, *A Textbook of Psychology* (Second Edition) (New York: W.B. Saunders Co., 1966).

20. Ibid., p. 195.

21. Ibid., pp. 195–96.

22. Ibid., p. 195, and *passim*.

23. Herbert Blumer, *Symbolic Interactionism: Perspective and Method* (Englewood Cliffs, N.J.: Prentice-Hall, 1969), p. 31.

24. Gilbert Ryle, *The Concept of Mind* (New York: Barnes & Noble, 1949) p. 33 *et. seq.*: Jerry Fodor, 'Logical Behaviorism' in his *The Language of Thought* (New York: Thomas Y. Crowell, 1975) pp. 2–9.

25. Fodor, *Language of Thought*, p. 8.

26. Of course, the question: 'What caused the clown *to be* clever?' might appear to be suitable for Fodor's kind of 'psychophysiological explanation'. Enough has been said, I hope, to show at least that (i) the appropriate sort of explanation of *that* does not require recourse to more than practical reasoning (itself investigable for its (informal) logic) and (ii) given that 'being clever' is an indexical predicate lacking anything remotely like a set of invariant recognitors it could not qualify as the subject of any nomothetic explanation at all: moreover, since any instance of 'being clever (witty, intelligent, etc.)' would have to consist in part of the performance of activities, and since no activity is definable purely in terms of bodily movements, appeals to brain events (whether computational or otherwise) could not satisfy the original demand for an answer to the question posed. Neither intelligence nor cleverness are 'natural kinds.'

Conclusion

In the bulk of these discussions, I have been attempting to come to terms with a beguiling but, I believe, fundamentally false theory of conduct and cognition; one which, as Haugeland has put it, takes as its 'guiding inspiration' the view that a theory of cognition 'should have the same basic form as the theories that explain sophisticated computer systems';[1] I have also been advancing some methodological and conceptual arguments in support of a sociologically-sensitive alternative to the rule of computationalism in cognitive studies. I am in full agreement with Heil who, in a recent paper on Fodor's metatheory for cognitive science,[2] argues as follows:

> we must take care to avoid the error of supposing that descriptions of things done are really *indirect* descriptions of the mechanisms which get them done. This is where the use of computer models of the activities of persons seems especially pernicious. To coax a computing machine to perform a certain task, we must first say what it is we want done. This requires that we describe in a precise way the performances we have in mind. Thus, the complexity of the programmes we write may well be a function of the complexity of the descriptions with which we are obliged to supply the computing machine. If we are successful, the machine will use our description (appropriately 'coded') to carry out the task we have set for it . . . . This, however, is simply a boring fact about the way in which we have programmed the machine. It scarcely licenses the conclusion that any device which performs the task in question necessarily does so in anything like the way the computing machine does it.[3]

And, on the issue of the role of neurophysiological data in assisting us in 'deciding' upon the putative 'psychophysiological realisation' of a preferred version of a grammar of a natural language, Whitaker and Whitaker[4] are succinct:

> The theoretical linguistic frameworks of aphasia studies have mirrored the various linguistic theories current in North America, Europe, and elsewhere; in practice, many of the studies are best described as informal structuralist approaches although some have been frankly tagmemic, stratificational, or transformational in orientation. Since the relationship between abstract linguistic theories and mental or performative grammars is not yet fully and precisely defined (Watt, 1974),[5] it is unrealistic to assume that aphasic language data could provide evidence supporting or disconfirming one or more of the current theories in linguistics.[6]

In other words, the thrust of a good deal of recent counter-argument against computationalist versions of cognitive science involves recognising the inadequacies of current attempts by psychologists to 'follow Putnam in treating the distinction between "brain process" and "mental process" as of no greater philosophical interest than that between "hardware description" and "description of the program" '.[7] Not only are there many *different* ways in which to codify aspects of human conduct in programming formats, but the very applicability of the concept of a 'program' to characterisations of *the mental* is itself arbitrary, and certainly not ordained by abstract appeals to properties of brain structure, any more than neurolinguistic research can buttress the claims of one or another linguist to have determined a 'mental' grammar.

In sum, then, I have been arguing that the computational and sentient-automata approach to the study of conduct, especially 'cognitive' conduct, is misleading as a source of conceptual tools and either false or incoherent as a way of overcoming the classical problems of the behavioural sciences with the concept of the mental.

The positive theses being advanced here draw heavily upon the conceptual-analytic tradition in logical and philosophical analysis and upon the empirical-analytic tradition in sociology called ethnomethodology. As *a priori* formalisms for the elucidation of the major properties of human conduct, these approaches have been most fruitful in revealing the extent to which the 'mental' domains of discourse and conceptualisation in everyday life are socially constructed and to what constraints their intelligibility is subject. (It should be noted that an *a priori* claim may be predicated upon the scrutiny of actual, worldly data of actions and interactions: Kripke has clearly shown that an *a priori* necessity can be derived from looking at the world as well as from 'unempirical' ratiocination.[8]) Of course, the analytical elucidation of the role of the 'mental' in practical affairs is at some distance from the orders of 'theorising' herein discussed. It remains unclear to what extent any meaningful 'theory' (as distinct from formal theorems, principles, etc.) can be developed from such a focus, but then premature theorising has not brought us appreciably closer to our goal of delivering coherent and defensible accounts of such matters as how memory works, how people make sense of one another, and so forth. That such matters are indeed studiable in terms of the practical details of ordinary, everyday affairs still strikes some as a very radical claim to make, but I think that this is, in part, a function of theoreticians' having lost sight of the essentially *mundane* character of remembering, forgetting, intending, thinking and the rest of the putatively cognitive domain. Once sight is lost of the mundane observability of such states of affairs, it becomes very easy to make the unwarranted leap and argue that such predicates label (albeit indirectly) neural, computational or 'mental' events, states and processes instead of signal states of affairs in the intersubjective world.

I would like to re-emphasise what I take to be a central point in my arguments which has to do with the nature of the phenomena taken to be the *explananda* of cognitive science: there is no way, logically, to recognise or describe any given case as a case of some intelligent performance, of 'remembering', of 'deciding', of 'computing', etc., independently of the context in which an agent is engaged in a line of conduct, and there are no recognition algorithms for contextual particulars conjoined to behavioural descriptions such that any given form of 'cognitive conduct' might be precisely defined over an explicit *set* of (necessary and sufficient) observational data. There is nothing *intrinsically* identifiable as a case of, e.g., 'remembering', 'doing X with intelligence', apart from a tacit assumption about the context of given (sequences of) conduct and the operative intelligibility principles of a culture. 'Mental' predicates are inextricably bound up with actions and contexts, and are socially avowable and assignable in conventionalised (albeit non-algorithmic) ways. If someone wishes to assert that re-focusing upon the observable world, and eschewing the postulation of 'unobservable phenomena' to explain that world in the manner of cognitivism, amounts to a revisionist form of behaviourism, then so be it. However, it seems to me to be abundantly clear that few actual behaviourists would adopt a view such as this under the auspices of any extant part of their research programmes. Classical as well as contemporary behaviourism was highly physicalist and a-cultural: the position being developed here is neither.

Another difficulty routinely overlooked in the cognitivist tradition is the illicit substitution of transparent descriptions for opaque descriptions in accounting for conduct. (Recall that a 'transparent' description is one true for the observer and not necessarily for the agent, whereas an 'opaque' description is one true for the agent and only possibly for the observer.) In claiming, as Fodor does, that 'learning a determination of the extension of the predicates involves learning that they fall under certain rules (i.e., truth rules)'[9], and claiming, as Putnam does in a strange concession to Chomsky, that '(the child) had already tumbled (if Washoe can, so can he!) to the fact that he needs to internalize structure-dependent notions [to try to understand English as his first language – JC]',[10] the fundamental fallacy of substituting transparent for opaque descriptions of what children may be said to be *doing* is committed. In Heil's terms, 'the danger is perhaps analogous to that run by anthropologists who employ descriptive vocabularies utterly foreign to the societies which they set out to describe: in both cases, the danger of generating artifacts in place of observations is the same.'[11]

The best way to avoid creating artefacts with lives of their own at the expense of the subject-matter of our field is assuredly not to settle for the chief rival artefacts of reductionist forms of behaviourism, but to return to the study of human *actions* and interactions as phenomena in their own right, whose properties and relations may be found to exhibit a discoverable orderliness at their own distinctive level. The variety of relationships which may be posited as holding between actions, bodily movements and CNS events can then be explored in the requisite detail without prior encumbrances from metaphorical theorising. I am convinced that this is the only way forward for serious students of cognition who are dissatisfied with the present state of behavioural science theory, although I am fully prepared to admit that showing its promise is a difficult undertaking. For one thing, gathering relevant and rich data (in the form of audio and video recordings and transcriptions) and engaging in a formal study of their properties is both time-consuming and risky in terms of analytical pay-offs. So far, however, the study of naturally occurring human activities has generated a sufficiently elaborate and stimulating series of theorems and principles to justify a cautious optimism. At least, that is how I read the contributions of the ethnomethodologists and the analytical philosophers of mind and action, and I would venture to speculate that the greater the interchanges between the two approaches, the more likely we are to develop more rigorous appreciations of the properties of conduct.

NOTES

1. John Haugeland, 'Semantic Engines: An Introduction to Mind Design' in his edited collection, *Mind Design* (Montgomery, Vermont: Bradford Books, 1981), p. 2.
2. John Heil, 'Does Cognitive Psychology Rest on a Mistake?' *Mind*, vol. XC, no. 359, July 1981.
3. Ibid., p. 327.

4. Haiganoosh Whitaker and Harry Whitaker, 'Language Disorders' in Ronald Wardhaugh and H. Douglas Brown (eds), *A Survey of Applied Linguistics* (Ann Arbor: University of Michigan Press, 1977). This paper contains an excellent overview of contemporary work on aphasia from a neurolinguistic point of view.

5. W.C. Watt, 'Mentalism in Linguistics 11', *Glossa*, vol. 8, 1974, as in Whitaker and Whitaker, 'Language Disorders'.

6. Whitaker and Whitaker, 'Language Disorders', p. 262.

7. Richard Rorty, 'Epistemology and Psychology' in his *Philosophy and the Mirror of Nature* (Princeton: Princeton University Press, 1979) p. 255. Rorty seems to endorse this view.

8. See the important discussion by Kripke in his celebrated essay, 'Naming and Necessity' in Donald Davidson and Gilbert Harman (eds), *Semantics of Natural Language* (Boston: D. Reidel, 1972), especially p. 261ff: 'They [some philosophers – JC] think that if something belongs to the realm of *a priori* knowledge, it couldn't possibly be known empirically. This is just a mistake. Something may belong in the realm of such statements that can be known *a priori* but still may be known by particular people on the basis of experience.' I would add that propositions in what I have termed 'conceptual phenomenology' may often have the form of synthetic *a prioris*. For a fuller discussion of the *a prioristic* character of various ethnomethodological propositions grounded upon real-worldly materials, see my 'Contingent and *A Priori* Structures in Sequential Analysis' in J.M. Atkinson and J.C. Heritage (eds), *Structures of Social Action* (forthcoming).

9. Jerry Fodor, *The Language of Thought* (New York: Thomas Y. Crowell, 1975), p. 63.

10. Hilary Putnam, 'What is Innate and Why. Comments on the Debate (between Jean Piaget and Noam Chomsky)' in Massimo Piattelli-Palmarini (ed.), *Language and Learning: The Debate between Jean Piaget and Noam Chomsky* (Cambridge, Mass: Harvard University Press, 1980) p. 294.

11. Heil, 'Cognitive Psychology', p. 326.

Bibliography

Anderson, John R., *Language, Memory and Thought* (New York: LEA/John Wiley, 1976)

Anderson, John R. and Bower, G.H., *Human Associative Memory* (Washington D.C.: Hemisphere, 1974)

Anderson, W.T., *Behavior in Painful Places*, unpublished Ph.D. Dissertation, Sociology Department, Boston University, 1982

Arbib, Michael A., *The Metaphorical Brain* (New York: John Wiley, 1972)

Atkinson, J.M., 'Societal Reactions to Suicide: The Role of Coroners' Definitions' in Stan Cohen (ed.), *Images of Deviance* (London: Penguin, 1972)

—— and J.C. Heritage (eds), *Structures of Social Action* (forthcoming)

Austin, J.L., *Philosophical Papers*, eds., J.O. Urmson and G.J. Warnock, (Oxford: Oxford University Press, 1970)

Baker, G.P. and P.M.S. Hacker, *Wittgenstein: Understanding and Meaning*, vol. 1 (Oxford: Blackwell/University of Chicago Press, 1980)

Baker, Lynne Rudder, 'Why Computers Can't Act', *American Philosophical Quarterly*, vol. 18, no. 2, April 1981

Bannister, D., 'The Logical Requirements for Research into Schizophrenia', *British Journal of Psychiatry*, vol. 114, no. 2, 1968

Becker, A.L. and Yengoyan, A.L. (eds), *The Imagination of Reality* (N.Y.: Ablex, 1979)

Begg, I. and Paivio, A., 'Concreteness and Imagery in Sentence Meaning', *Journal of Verbal Learning and Verbal Behavior*, vol. 8, 1969

Berger, Peter and Luckmann, Thomas, *The Social Construction of Reality* (London: Allen Lane, Penguin Press, 1967)

Bernstein, Richard J., *The Restructuring of Social and Political Theory* (Philadelphia: University of Pennsylvania Press, 1978)

Black, Max, 'Comment on Chomsky's "Explanation in Linguistic Theory" ' in R. Borger and F. Cioffi (eds), *Explanation in the Behavioral Sciences* (Cambridge: Cambridge University Press, 1970)

Block, Ned, 'What is Philosophy of Psychology?' in N. Block (ed.), *Readings in Philosophy of Psychology* (Cambridge, Mass.: Harvard University Press, 1980)

—— (ed.), *Readings in Philosophy of Psychology* (Cambridge, Mass.: Harvard University Press, 1980)

—— and Dworkin, Gerald, 'I.Q., Heritability and Inequality' in N.J. Block and Gerald Dworkin, eds, *The I.Q. Controversy* (Pantheon Books, Random House, 1976)

Blumer, Herbert, *Symbolic Interactionism: Perspective and Method* (New Jersey: Prentice-Hall, 1969).

Bobrow, D.G., 'Natural Language Input for a Computer Problem-Solving System' in M. Minsky, ed., *Semantic Information Processing* (Cambridge, Mass.: M.I.T. Press, 1968)

Boden, Margaret, *Artificial Intelligence and Natural Man* (New York, Basic Books, 1977)

Booth, D.A., 'Protein Synthesis and Memory' in J.A. Deutsch (ed.), *The Physiological Basis of Memory* (New York: Academic Press, 1973)

Borger, R. and Frank Cioffi, eds, *Explanation in the Behavioral Sciences* (Cambridge University Press, 1970)

Borst, C.V., ed., *The Mind/Brain Identity Theory* (London: Macmillan, 1970)

Brewer, William F., 'There is No Convincing Evidence for Operant or Classical Conditioning in Adult Humans' in Walter B. Weimer and D.S. Palermo, (eds), *Cognition and the Symbolic Processes* (New York: Erlbaum/Halsted/John Wiley, 1974)

——, 'The Problem of Meaning and the Interrelations of the Higher Mental Processes' in Weimer & Palermo, eds, *Cognition and the Symbolic Processes* (New York: Erlbaum/Halstead/John Wiley, 1974)

——, 'Memory for Ideas: Synonym Substitutions', unpublished MSS, University of Illinois, 1974

Brill, N.Q. and Glass, J.F., 'Hebephrenic Schizophrenic Reactions', *Archives of General Psychiatry*, vol. 12, no. 1, 1965

Brillouin, L., *Science and Information Theory* (New York: Academic Press, 1956)

Buchsbaum, Monte S., 'Psychophysiology and Schizophrenia', *Schizophrenia Bulletin* (N.I.M.H.), vol. 3, no. 1, 1977

Bunge, Mario, 'From Neuron to Behavior and Mentation: An Exercise in Levelmanship' in H.M. Pinsker and W.D. Willis Jnr., eds, *Information Processing and the Nervous System* (New York: Raven Press, 1980)

Bursen, H.A., *Dismantling the Memory Machine: A Philosophical Investigation of Machine Theories of Memory* (Dordrecht: Reidel, 1978)

Butler, R.J. (ed.), *Analytical Philosophy, vols 1 and 2* (Oxford: Blackwell, 1965)

Carpenter Jnr., W.T. *et al.*, 'Another View of Schizophrenic Subtypes', *Archives of General Psychiatry*, vol. 33, no. 1, 1976

Carroll, Lewis, 'What the Tortoise Said to Achilles', *Complete Works* (London: Nonesuch Press, n.d.)

Castaneda, Hector-Neri (ed.), *Intentionality, Mind and Perception* (Detroit: Wayne State University Press, 1966)

Chapouthier, Georges, 'Behavioral Studies of the Molecular Basis of Memory' in J.A. Deutsch (ed.), *The Physiological Basis of Memory* (1973)

Chisholm, Roderick W., 'Responsibility and Avoidability' in Sidney Hook (ed.), *Determinism and Freedom in the Age of Modern Science* (New York: Collier Books, 1961)

Chomsky, Noam, 'Review of B.F. Skinner's *Verbal Behavior*', *Language*, vol. 35, no. 1, 1959

——, *Current Issues in Linguistic Theory* (The Hague: Mouton, 1964)

——, 'Explanation in Linguistic Theory' in R. Borger & F. Cioffi (eds), *Explanation in the Behavioral Sciences* (Cambridge: Cambridge University Press, 1970)

——, *Reflections on Language* (New York: Pantheon Books, 1975)

——, 'Reply to Critics', *Behavioral and Brain Sciences*, vol. 3, no. 1, March 1980

Churchland, Pamela S., 'A Perspective on Mind-Brain Research', *Journal of Philosophy*, vol. 77, no. 4, April 1980

Cicourel, Aaron V., *Cognitive Sociology* (Harmondsworth: Penguin, 1973)

Cohen, Stan (ed.), *Images of Deviance* (London: Penguin, 1972)

Cook-Gumperz, Jenny, 'The Child as Practical Reasoner' in M. Sanches and B. Blount (eds), *Sociocultural Dimensions of Language Use* (New York: Academic Press, 1975)

Cooper, David E., *Knowledge of Language* (New York: Humanities Press, 1975)

Coulter, Jeff, 'The Brain as Agent', *Human Studies*, vol. 2, no. 4, October 1979

——, *The Social Construction of Mind* (London: Macmillan, 1979)

——, 'Theoretical Problems of Cognitive Science', *Inquiry*, vol. 25, no. 1, 1982

Davidson, Donald, 'Mental Events' in Ned Block (ed.), *Readings in Philosophy of Psychology* (Cambridge, Mass.: Harvard University Press, 1980)

—— and Harman, Gilbert (eds), *Semantics of Natural Language* (Reidel, Humanities Press, 1972)

Dennett, Daniel C., *Brainstorms: Philosophical Essays on Mind and Psychology* (Vermont: Bradford Books, 1978)

Deutsch, J.A. (ed.), *The Physiological Basis of Memory* (New York: Academic Press, 1973)

Douglas, Jack D., (ed.), *Understanding Everyday Life: Toward the Reconstruction of Sociological Knowledge* (Chicago: Aldine, 1970)

—— (ed.), *Deviance and Respectability: The Social Construction of Moral Meanings* (New York: Basic Books, 1970)

Dretske, Fred I., *Knowledge and the Flow of Information* (Cambridge, Mass.: M.I.T. Press, 1981)

Dreyfus, H.L., *Alchemy and Artificial Intelligence* (Santa Monica, California: Rand Corporation, 1965)

——, *What Computers Can't Do: A Critique of Artificial Reason* (New York: Harper & Row, 1972)

Drury, M. O'C., 'Conversations with Wittgenstein' in Rush Rhees (ed.), *Ludwig Wittgenstein: Personal Recollections* (New Jersey: Rowman & Littlefield, 1981)

Duncan, S. and Fiske, D., *Face-to-Face Interaction: Research, Methods and Theory* (New Jersey: Erlbaum, 1977)

Eccles, Sir John, *The Neurophysiological Basis of Mind: Principles of Neurophysiology* (Oxford: Clarendon Press, 1953)

——, *The Understanding of the Brain* (New York: McGraw-Hill, 1973)

Feyerabend, Paul, *Against Method* (New York: Verso/Schocken Books, 1980)

Fodor, Jerry A., *Psychological Explanation* (New York: Random House, 1968)

——, *The Language of Thought* (New York: Thomas Crowell, 1975)

Garfinkel, Harold, *Studies in Ethnomethodology* (Englewood Cliffs, N.J.: Prentice-Hall, 1967)

Gerard, Ralph W., 'What Is Memory?' in *Psychobiology* (San Francisco: Scientific American: W.H. Freeman, 1967)

Goffman, Erving, *Relations in Public* (New York: Basic Books, 1971)

Goode, David, 'The World of the Congenitally Deaf-Blind' in Howard Schwartz and Jerry Jacobs (eds), *Qualitative Sociology: A Method to the Madness*

(New York: Free Press, 1979)

Granit, Ragnar, *The Purposive Brain* (Cambridge Mass: M.I.T. Press, 1977)

Gregory, Richard, *Eye and Brain* (London: Weidenfeld & Nicolson, 1977 edn)

Harrison, Bernard, *Meaning and Structure: An Essay in the Philosophy of Language* (New York: Harper & Row, 1972)

Haugeland, John, 'Semantic Engines' in J. Haugeland (ed.), *Mind Design* (Vermont: Bradford Books, 1981)

Hebb, D.O., *A Textbook of Psychology*, second edition (New York: W.B. Saunders, 1966)

Heil, John, 'Does Cognitive Psychology Rest on a Mistake?' *Mind*, vol. XC, no. 359, July 1981

Helm, David, 'Conferring Membership: Interacting with "Incompetents",' unpublished Ph.D. Dissertation, Sociology Department, Boston University, 1981

Henslin, James M. 'Guilt and Guilt Neutralization: Response and Adjustment to Suicide' in J.D. Douglas (ed.), *Deviance and Respectability* (New York: Basic Books, 1970)

Holborow, Les, 'The "Prejudice" in Favor of Psychophysical Parallelism' in Godfrey Vesey (ed.), *Understanding Wittgenstein: The Royal Institute of Philosophy Lectures, vol. 7 (1972–73)*, (London: Macmillan, 1974)

Honderich, Ted (ed.), *Essays on Freedom of Action* (London: Routledge & Kegan Paul, 1973)

Hook, Sidney (ed.), *Determinism and Freedom in the Age of Modern Science* (New York: Collier Books, 1961)

Hunter, John F.M., ' "Forms of Life" in Wittgenstein's *Philosophical Investigations*' in E.D. Klemke (ed.), *Essays on Wittgenstein* (Urbana: University of Illinois Press, 1971)

——, 'On How We Talk' in his *Essays After Wittgenstein* (Toronto: University of Toronto Press, 1973)

——, 'Wittgenstein and Materialism', *Mind*, vol. 86, no. 344, October 1977

John, E.R., *Mechanisms of Memory* (New York: Academic Press, 1967)

Kant, I., *Critique of Pure Reason*, trans. N.K. Smith (London: Macmillan, 1964 edn)

Katz, M.M. *et al.*, 'Non-specificity of Diagnosis of Paranoid Schizophrenia', *Archives of General Psychiatry*, vol. 11, no. 2, 1964

Kendell, R.E., *The Role of Diagnosis in Psychiatry* (Oxford: Blackwell Scientific Publications, 1975)

Kenny, A.J.P., *Will, Freedom and Power* (Oxford: Blackwell, 1976)

Kety, Seymour S., 'Heredity and Environment' in John C. Shershow (ed.), *Schizophrenia: Science and Practice* (Cambridge, Mass.: Harvard University Press, 1978)

——, 'Prospects for Research in Schizophrenia: An Overview' in Francis O. Schmitt *et al.* (eds), *Neurosciences Research Symposium Summaries, vol. 7* (Cambridge, Mass.: M.I.T. Press, 1973)

Kim, Jaegwon, 'On the Psychophysical Identity Theory', *American Philosophical Quarterly*, vol. 3, 1966

Klemke, E.D. (ed.), *Essays on Wittgenstein* (Urbana: University of Illinois Press, 1971)

Klerman, Gerald L., 'The Evolution of a Scientific Nosology' in John C. Shershow (ed.), *Schizophrenia: Science and Practice* (Cambridge, Mass.: Harvard University Press, 1978)

Kohlberg, L., 'Stage and Sequence: The Cognitive Development Approach to Socialisation' in D. Goslin (ed.), *Handbook of Theory and Research in Socialization* (Chicago: Rand-McNally, 1969)

Krech, D., 'Discussion' in J.L. McGough (ed.), *Advances in Behavioral Biology, vol. 4* (New York: Plenum Press, 1972)

Kripke, Saul, 'Naming and Necessity' in Donald Davidson and Gilbert Harman (eds), *Semantics of Natural Language* (Boston: Reidel, 1972)

Kuhn, Thomas S., *The Structure of Scientific Revolutions* (International Encyclopoedia of Unified Science: University of Chicago Press, 1970)

Kvale, Steinar, 'The Temporality of Memory', *Journal of Phenomenological Psychology*, vol. 5, no. 1, Fall 1974

Lansing, J.S., 'In the World of the Sea Urchin' in A.L. Becker and A.L. Yengoyan (eds), *The Imagination of Reality* (New York: Ablex, 1979)

Lashley, K.S., 'In Search of the Engram', *Symposia of the Society for Experimental Biology*, vol. 4, no. 1, 1950

Leinfeller , E. *et al.* (eds), *Wittgenstein and his Impact on Contemporary Thought* (Proceedings of the Second International Wittgenstein Symposium: Vienna: Holder-Pichler-Tempsky, 1978)

Lettvin, J.Y., H. Maturana, W.S. McCulloch and W.H. Pitts, 'What the Frog's Eye Tells the Frog's Brain', *Proceedings IRE*, vol. 47, 1959

Luce, David Randall, 'Mind-Body Identity and Psycho-Physical Correlation', *Philosophical Studies*, vol. 17, no. 3, 1966

Macleod, R.B., 'Phenomenology: A Challenge to Experimental Psychology' in T.W. Wann (ed.), *Behaviorism and Phenomenology: Contrasting Bases for Modern Psychology* (Phoenix: University of Chicago Press, 1967)

Malcolm, Norman, 'Explaining Behavior', *The Philosophical Review*, vol. 76, no. 2, January 1967

——, 'The Myth of Cognitive Processes and Structures' in T. Mischel (ed.), *Cognitive Development and Epistemology* (New York: Academic Press, 1971)

——, *Memory and Mind* (Ithaca, New York and London: Cornell University Press, 1977)

——, 'Thinking' in E. Leinfeller *et al.* (eds), *Wittgenstein and his Impact on Contemporary Thought* (Vienna: Holder-Pichler-Tempsky, 1978)

McConnell, J.V. *et al*, 'Attempts to Transfer Approach and Avoidance Responses by RNA Injection in Rats', *Journal of Biological Psychology*, vol. 10, no. 2, 1964

McGinn, Colin, 'Anomalous Monism and Kripke's Cartesian Intuitions' in Ned Block (ed.), *Readings in Philosophy of Psychology* (Cambridge, Mass.: Harvard University Press, 1980)

McGough, J.L. (ed.), *Advances in Behavioral Biology, vol. 4* (New York: Plenum Press, 1972)

Melden, A.I., 'Willing' in Alan R. White (ed.), *The Philosophy of Action* (Oxford: Oxford University Press, 1968)

Minsky, Marvin (ed.), *Semantic Information Processing* (Cambridge, Mass.: M.I.T. Press, 1968)

Mischel, Theodore, 'Conceptual Issues in the Psychology of the Self' in Theodore Mischel (ed.), *The Self: Psychological and Philosophical Issues* (Oxford: Basil Blackwell, 1977)

Mucciolo, L.F., 'The Identity Theory and Neuropsychology', *Nous*, vol. 8, 1974

Munoz, R.A. *et al*, 'Simple and Hebephrenic Schizophrenia: A Follow-up Study' in M. Roff *et al* (eds), *Life History Research in Psychopathology, vol. 2* (Minneapolis: University of Minnesota Press, 1972)

Munsat, Stanley, *The Concept of Memory* (New York: Random House, 1967)

Nagel, Thomas, 'Physicalism', *The Philosophical Review*, vol. 74, no. 2, 1965

—— , 'What is it Like to be a Bat?' in Ned Block (ed.), *Readings in Philosophy of Psychology, vol. 1* (Cambridge, Mass.: Harvard University Press, 1980)

Neisser, Ulrich, *Cognitive Psychology* (New York: Appleton, 1967)

Neustein, Amy, *Courtroom Examination: An Analysis of its Formal Properties*, unpublished Ph.D. Dissertation, Sociology Department, Boston University, 1982

Palermo, David S., 'Is A Scientific Revolution Taking Place in Psychology?' *Science Studies*, vol. 1, no. 1, 1971

Papert, Seymour, *The Artificial Intelligence of Hubert L. Dreyfus* (Cambridge, Mass.: M.I.T. AI Lab., 1968)

Parsons, Talcott and Bales, Robert F., *Family Socialisation and Interaction Process* (New York: Free Press, 1955)

Pears, David, *Wittgenstein* (London: Fontana Modern Masters, 1971)

Pinsker, H.M. and Willis, W.D., Jnr (eds), *Information Processing and the Nervous System* (New York: Raven Press, 1980)

Pitkin, Hanna F., *Wittgenstein and Justice: On the Significance of Ludwig Wittgenstein for Social and Political Thought* (Los Angeles, Calif.: University of California Press, 1972)

Polanyi, Michael, *Personal Knowledge* (Phoenix: University of Chicago Press, 1958)

Putnam, Hilary, 'Minds and Machines' in Sidney Hook (ed.), *Dimensions of Mind* (London: Collier-Macmillan, 1960)

—— , 'Brains and Behavior' in R.J. Butler (ed.), *Analytical Philosophy, vol. 2* (Oxford: Blackwell, 1965)

—— , 'The Mental Life of Some Machines' in H.-N. Castaneda, (ed.), *Intentionality, Minds and Perception* (Detroit: Wayne State University Press, 1966)

—— , 'What is Innate and Why' in Massimo Piattelli-Palmarini, (ed.), *Language and Learning: The Debate Between Jean Piaget and Noam Chomsky* (Cambridge, Mass.: Harvard University Press, 1980)

Pylyshyn, Zenon, 'Mind, Machines and Phenomenology', *Cognition*, vol. 3, no. 1, 1974–75

—— , 'Computation and Cognition: Issues in the Foundation of Cognitive Science', *The Behavioral and Brain Sciences*, vol. 3, no. 1, March 1980

Quine, Willard V.O., *Word and Object* (Cambridge, Mass.: M.I.T. Press, 1960)

—— , 'The Inscrutability of Reference' in Danny D. Steinberg and Leon A. Jakobovits (eds), *Semantics* (Cambridge: Cambridge University Press, 1971)

—— , 'Methodological Reflections on Current Linguistic Theory' in Donald Davidson and Gilbert Harman (eds), *Semantics of Natural Language* (Boston and New York: Reidel, Humanities Press, 1972)

Richter, Derek (ed.), *Aspects of Learning and Memory* (New York: Basic Books, 1966)

Rorty, Richard, 'Wittgensteinian Philosophy and Empirical Psychology', *Philosophical Studies*, vol. 31, no. 3, 1977

——, *Philosophy and the Mirror of Nature* (Princeton: Princeton University Press, 1979)

Ryle, Gilbert, *The Concept of Mind* (New York: Barnes and Noble, 1949)

Sacks, Harvey, *Aspects of the Sequential Organisation of Conversation*, unpublished MSS, University of California at Irvine, School of Social Sciences, n.d.

——, 'Some Technical Considerations of a Dirty Joke' in Jim Schenkein (ed.), *Studies in the Organisation of Conversational Interaction* (New York: Academic Press, 1978)

——, Schegloff, E.A. and Jefferson, G., 'A Simplest Systematics for the Organization of Turn-Taking for Conversation', *Language*, vol. 50, no. 4, part 1, December 1974

Sanches M. and Blount, B., (eds), *Sociocultural Dimensions of Language Use* (New York: Academic Press, 1975)

Schenkein, Jim (ed.), *Studies in the Organisation of Conversational Interaction* (New York: Academic Press, 1978)

Schmitt, Francis O. *et al* (eds), *Neurosciences Research Symposium Summaries, Vol. 7* (Cambridge, Mass.: M.I.T. Press, 1973)

Schutz, Alfred, *The Phenomenology of the Social World*, trans. George Walsh and Frederick Lehnert (USA: Northwestern University Press, 1967)

Schwartz, Howard and Jacobs, Jerry, *Qualitative Sociology: A Method to the Madness* (New York: Free Press, 1979)

Searle, John, *Expression and Meaning* (Cambridge: Cambridge University Press, 1979)

——, 'Minds, Brains and Programs', *The Behavioral and Brain Sciences*, vol. 3, no. 3, September 1980

——, 'Intrinsic Intentionality', *The Behavioral and Brain Sciences*, vol. 3, no. 3, September 1980

Shershow, John C. (ed.), *Schizophrenia: Science and Practice* (Cambridge, Mass.: Harvard University Press, 1978)

Shoemaker, Sydney, 'Functionalism and Qualia' in Ned Block (ed.), *Readings in Philosophy of Psychology*, vol. 1, 1980

Spear, Norman E., *The Processing of Memories: Forgetting and Retention* (New York: LEA/John Wiley, 1978)

Squires, Roger, 'Memory Unchained', *Philosophical Review*, vol. 78, April 1969

Steinberg, Danny D. and Jakobovits, Leon A., (eds), *Semantics* (Cambridge: Cambridge University Press, 1971)

Stephens, J.H., 'Long-Term Prognosis and Follow-up in Schizophrenia', *Schizophrenia Bulletin* (N.I.M.H.), vol. 4, no. 1, 1978

Stevens, Leonard A., *Explorers of the Brain* (New York: Knopf, 1971)

Stone, A.A. *et al*, 'Simple Schizophrenia: Syndrome or Shibboleth?' *American Journal of Psychiatry*, vol. 125, 1968

Strawson, Peter F., *Individuals: An Essay in Descriptive Metaphysics* (London: Methuen, 1959)

Thorp, John, *Free Will: A Defence Against Neurophysiological Determinism* (London: Routledge & Kegan Paul, 1980)

Valenstein, Elliot S., *Brain Control: A Critical Examination of Brain Stimulation and Psychosurgery* (New York: John Wiley, 1973)

Vesey, Godfrey (ed.), *Understanding Wittgenstein* (London: Macmillan, 1974)

Von Uexküll, Baron J.J., *Umwelt und Innenwelt der Tiere* (Berlin: Springer, 1909)

Waismann, Friedrich, *The Principles of Linguistic Philosophy*, ed. Rom Harré (London: Macmillan, 1965)

Wann, T W (ed.), *Behaviorism and Phenomenology: Contrasting Bases for Modern Psychology* (Phoenix: University of Chicago Press, 1967)

Warnock, G.J., *The Object of Morality* (London: Methuen, 1971)

Watt, W.C., 'Mentalism in Linguistics 11', *Glossa*, vol. 8, no. 2, 1974

Weil, Vivian M., 'Intentional and Mechanistic Explanation', *Philosophy and Phenomenological Research*, vol. XL, September 1979 – June 1980

Weimer, Walter B. and Palermo, David S. (eds), *Cognition and the Symbolic Processes* (New York: Erlbaum/Halsted/John Wiley, 1974)

Weizenbaum, Joseph, *Computer Power and Human Reason: From Judgment to Calculation* (San Francisco: W.H. Freeman, 1976)

Whitaker, Haiganoosh and Whitaker, Harry, 'Language Disorders' in Ronald Wardhaugh and H. Douglas Brown (eds), *A Survey of Applied Linguistics* (Ann Arbor: University of Michigan Press, 1977)

White, Alan R. (ed.), *The Philosophy of Action* (Oxford: Oxford University Press, 1968)

Wieder, D. Lawrence, 'On Meaning By Rule' in Jack D. Douglas (ed.), *Understanding Everyday Life* (Chicago: Aldine, 1970)

——, *Language and Social Reality: The Case of Telling the Convict Code* (The Hague: Mouton, 1975)

——, 'Behavioristic Operationalism and the Life-World. Chimpanzees and Chimpanzee Researchers in Face-to-Face Interaction', *Sociological Inquiry*, vol. 50 nos 3–4, 1980

Wiggins, David, 'Towards a Reasonable Libertarianism' in Ted Honderich (ed.), *Essays on Freedom of Action* (London: Routledge & Kegan Paul, 1973)

——, 'Identity, Designation, Essentialism, and Physicalism', *Philosophia*, vol. 5, 1975

Winch, Peter, *The Idea of a Social Science and Its Relation to Philosophy* (London: Routledge & Kegan Paul, 1958)

Wing, J.K. *et al*, *The Measurement and Classification of Psychiatric Symptoms* (Cambridge: Cambridge University Press, 1974)

Winograd, Terry, *Understanding Natural Language* (New York: Academic Press, 1972)

Wittgenstein, Ludwig, *Zettel* trans. G.E.M. Anscombe: eds, G.E.M. Anscombe and G.H. von Wright (Oxford: Basil Blackwell, 1967)

——, *Philosophical Investigations*, trans. G.E.M. Anscombe (Oxford: Basil Blackwell, 1968)

——, *Remarks on the Foundations of Mathematics*, eds, G.H. von Wright, Rush Rhees and G.E.M. Anscombe; trans. G.E.M. Anscombe (Cambridge, Mass.: M.I.T. Press, 1972)

——, *On Certainty*, eds G.E.M. Anscombe and G.H. von Wright: trans. D. Paul and G.E.M. Anscombe, (Oxford: Basil Blackwell, 1974)

Zimmerman, Don H., 'The Practicalities of Rule Use' in Jack D. Douglas (ed.), *Understanding Everyday Life* (Chicago: Aldine, 1970)

—— and Pollner, Melvin, 'The Everyday World as a Phenomenon' in Jack D. Douglas (ed.), *Understanding Everyday Life* (Chicago: Aldine, 1970)

Subject Index

Name Index

(Italicised numerals refer to the Notes)

177